MANY GIFTS ONE SPIRIT

REPORT OF ACC−7: SINGAPORE 1987

Published for the Anglican Consultative Council

Published 1987 for the Anglican Consultative Council, 14 Great Peter Street, London SW1P 3NQ

This edition by
Church House Publishing,
Church House, Great Smith Street,
London SW1P 3NZ

ISBN 0 7151 4764 1

Printed by Orphans Press Ltd., Leominster, Herefordshire. Tel. 2460.

Contents

One Lord, One Faith, One Baptism.

一主一信洗

Preface

MANY GIFTS, ONE SPIRIT

Each of the churches of the Anglican Communion claims only to be 'part of the one, Holy, Catholic and Apostolic Church'. Even the Communion as a whole does not claim to be more than *a part* of the Universal Church of Christ. Successive Lambeth Conferences have expressed the hope that the life of the Communion would be subsumed ultimately in the larger fellowship of a reunited church of Christ. Anglicans in the South Asian subcontinent have actually taken the decision to unite with Christians of other traditions. Since the adoption of the Chicago-Lambeth Quadrilateral by the 1888 Lambeth Conference, Anglicans have been open to negotiations for union with other Christian traditions with the Quadrilateral as a basis for discussion. This ecumenical aspect of Anglicanism was in high profile at ACC-7. Surrounding the Compasrose, the symbol of world-wide Anglicanism, in the Plenary Hall and Chapel were the Chinese characters for 'One Lord, One Faith, One Baptism'. The Secretary General in his review reminded the Council of the Communion's commitment to ecumenism. The Council benefited greatly from major plenary addresses by Christians from other traditions – Dr Alan Boesak of the World Alliance of Reformed Churches, Professor Nicholas Lash from the Roman Catholic Church and Dr Harding Meyer from the Lutheran Church.

The report of the ecumenical section recommended that membership of the Council of those churches which have come into existence as a result of Anglicans uniting with Christians of other traditions, should move from being token membership to normal membership. While Anglicans remain committed to ecumenism, they have become increasingly conscious of the world-wide nature of the Anglican Communion and are feeling the need to develop structures which reflect this reality. A paper, prepared by a small group under the chairmanship of the Archbishop of Armagh, outlined four instruments for maintaining the 'unity in diversity' of the Anglican Communion. These are, the Archbishop of Canterbury, who is described as 'the personal symbol of unity' in the Communion, the Lambeth Conference, which is recognised as a valuable forum where 'the mind of the churches' is discerned and expressed, and the Anglican Consultative Council itself, which is representative of the clergy and laity as well as the episcopate. While retaining its consultative nature, it was felt that it should 'reflect more closely the pattern of representation on synodical bodies at local and provincial levels'. Finally, there is the Primates' Meeting which provides opportunities for collegiality between those having special responsibility in individual provinces. It was suggested that there might be closer liaison

vii

between the ACC and the Primates' Meeting. The Council received with gratitude a new book of essays *Authority in the Anglican Communion,* edited by Professor Stephen Sykes, and found it extremely helpful in their discussion of Anglican structures.

The world-wide nature of the Anglican Communion means that Anglicans increasingly find themselves in very diverse cultural, socio-economic and political situations. The inculturation of the Gospel in these very different situations is, therefore, a matter of some urgency. Anglicanism has traditionally emphasised the authority of the local church in ordaining, changing or abolishing ceremonies or rites of the church 'ordained only by man's authority' (article 34). As a matter of fact, Anglicans have sometimes been hesitant to create patterns of worship and of ministry which are culturally appropriate. This is now changing and part of the mandate given to the newly recommended Liturgical Commission is to 'study and reflect on those areas in which inculturation and contextualisation of Anglican worship is developing'. The Council welcomed the report *For the Sake of the Kingdom,* recognising that there are aspects of every culture which can be affirmed by Christians just as there are other aspects which are challenged by the Gospel.

The diverse contexts in which contemporary Anglicanism finds itself are often religious as well as culturally plural. Anglicans have to learn to live with people of other faiths and of no faith. The Council recognised the importance of people of different faiths co-operating in nation building activities and in the achievement of social and political harmony. Christians should be concerned about human rights, including the right to freedom of belief. Inter-religious dialogue will invariably involve Christians in seeking to understand the beliefs and practices of their non-Christian neighbours. During the course of dialogue, Christians will discover certain commonalities with others, they will also discover serious and deep differences. If dialogue is to continue, there must be continued mutual respect and openness despite the discovery of differences. The Council was concerned to warn Christians of superstitious and occult elements in many cultural and religious traditions, recognising that at times such elements were to be found even among Christians. The *Peace and Justice* and the *Family and Community* Networks had met just before the Council. The Council's deliberations on questions of personal and public morality, distributive justice, war, racism, relations between the sexes and other such matters were influenced by the weighty reports of the two Networks to the Council. The Council passed a strong resolution on apartheid condemming it as an 'evil, racist system'. It called upon member churches to press their governments and business and financial institutions in their area to pursue a policy of disengagement with South Africa as long as its government continues with its present policies. In the context of Arab-Israeli relations, the Council, while recognising Israel's right to exist within secure borders, affirmed the importance of the Church's role in promoting justice for all. In particular, it recognised the injustice done to the Palestinian people and affirmed their right to self-determination.

On AIDS, the Council pointed out that the disease is largely spread as a consequence of life-styles. It urged everyone to uphold fidelity within marriage and abstinence outside it. It recognised, however, that there will be many who do not uphold the standards set by the Church. State and voluntary agencies will need to warn them of the dangers and to advise them on precautions they need to take. It urged that special pastoral concern be shown by the Church for those with AIDS and for their families. It welcomed the publication of guide-lines for pastoral care by various churches and urged that such guide-lines be widely used. Pastoral care should not be left to the clergy alone but should involve a cross-section of the local Christian community.

The emergence of Networks, such as *Peace and Justice* and the *Family and Community* Networks within the Anglican Communion was seen as a significant development in the last few years. The Council asked its Standing Committee to appoint a working party which would prepare guidelines for the establishment and operation of Networks.

The New Testament reading set for the opening service from 1 Cor. 12 had reminded us that in God's Church there are many gifts but the same Spirit. We were deeply conscious of this reality throughout ACC-7. The Council provided us with a forum where these different gifts could be shared with each other in fellowship and in mutual charity.

The Archbishop of Canterbury had said in his opening sermon that we should always be ready to recognise all God's gifts in all God's people and that the Church should always be willing to recognise new gifts which God graciously gives to his people. That is just what we tried to do at Singapore!

Resolutions of the Seventh Meeting of the Anglican Consultative Council

GENERAL BUSINESS

PART 1 – INTRODUCTORY ADDRESSES

Archbishop of Canterbury's Introduction

The following is the Archbishop of Canterbury's Address to ACC Members at the opening of the ACC-7 Meeting in Singapore.

There is no tradition of a Presidential address at this Assembly but it falls to me as the President of the ACC to welcome you all to this 7th meeting of the Anglican Consultative Council. As Archbishop of Canterbury I frequently welcome people to meetings which others have largely prepared. My welcome to you this morning is all the more sincere because of the debt of gratitude we owe to others who have worked so hard to make our meeting here in Singapore spiritually constructive for the communion and physically comfortable for its delegated representatives.

My first task in welcoming you all is to introduce the Members who are attending the Council for the first time. It is rather a long list; but I think we should ask each to stand briefly so that we can identify you, in alphabetical order as befits a democratic gathering. Forgive me in silence, or use the chance to protest, if I mispronounce your name.

> Mr Justice Christian Abimbola – Nigeria
> Mr Edgar Bradley – New Zealand
> Bishop Luke Chhoa – East Asia
> Bishop Din Dayal – North India
> Bishop Drexel Gomez – West Indies
> Mrs. Betty Govinden – Southern Africa
> Archbishop Douglas Hambidge – Canada
> Miss Lorna Helen – Ireland
> Bishop Colin James – England
> Bishop Andrew Kumarage – Sri Lanka
> Dr. Julio Lozano – Southern Cone of America
> The Revd Bernard Malango – Central Africa
> The Revd John Makokwe – Burundi, Rwanda and Zaire
> Mr David McIntyre – Wales
> Bishop Patrice Njojo – Burundi, Rwanda and Zaire
> Archbishop George Noakes – Wales
> Bishop James Ottley – ECUSA
> Archbishop Donald Robinson – Australia
> Bishop Sumio Takatsu – Brazil
> Mr John Tealiklava – Melanesia
> The Revd Louis Tsui – East Asia

Canon Ian Watt – Scotland
Mrs Ruth Yansoon-Choi – East Asia
Bishop Daniel Zindo – Sudan

I would also like to welcome the Observers from other Churches:

Dr Jonas Jonson – Lutheran World Federation
Bishop Philopose Mar Chrysostom – Mar Thoma Syrian Church of
   Malabar
Bishop Gerhard A. Van Kleef – Union of Utrecht
The Revd John Chryssavgis – Orthodox Church
Fr Kevin McDonald – Roman Catholic Church
Mr William Thompson – World Council of Churches
The Revd Dr Stephen C. Tan – World Alliance of Reformed Churches

Within the Anglican Communion we increasingly recognize that we cannot find the answers to some of the great questions which face us without reference to other World Christian Communions. You too are facing questions of authority, mission and ministry. We need each other in their resolution. That is why you are here and the Council warmly welcomes your presence and anticipates your fullest participation.

I welcome our Consultants. Professional theologians and those with special first-hand experience of the subjects under discussion are essential. We live in a climate which is suspicious of experts. But we look to our Consultants to deliver us from seductive false simplicities and to provide us with that essential element of repentance and self-criticism. No doubt you will also offer us your share of midnight drafting.

We all bring to meetings a variety of recent experiences. I have already been taking part in the Standing Committee of the Council, and on my arrival on Thursday, two Inter-Anglican Networks were already in deliberation. At dinner I found myself caught up – not to say ensnared – in the Peace and Justice Network. This brought home to me not only the existence of the Networks but also the fact that their considerable expertise is offered to this council without direct cost on its budget. I am sure my Prime Minister, Mrs Thatcher, will be pleased to hear me praise them. They are remarkable expressions of private enterprise to set against any tendency towards bureaucratic centralism. All the sections in which we shall be working in the coming two weeks will owe much to the preliminary work of the various Networks and it is right that we should acknowledge this debt with some praise and gratitude.

I think we are all grateful to those provinces and publications which have helped us to have a team of professional Church communicators at this meeting; and they hope, in an imaginative way, to assemble a representative

Anglican and Ecumenical Communications Team for the Lambeth Conference 1988.

The Chairman will talk about the staff of the ACC. But when we think about staff-work my mind naturally turns to the colourful and courageous member of my own staff who has been such a character at the two ACC meetings we have attended together. We have all been praying for him in the last two months; and I know that Council members are anxious about him. I cannot give you any hard news about Terry Waite at the moment but that does not mean that we are doing nothing. Every rumour from Beirut and elsewhere is being followed up, every story checked, every political and religious contact used. But for the moment we still wait.

Perhaps it may be as well for me to remind members of the Council how a member of my staff responsible for Anglican Communion affairs became the envoy of the Archbishop of Canterbury in the dangerous business of negotiating for the release of hostages.

You will remember the situation in Iran after the revolution. For various reasons, mostly to do with the settling of old local scores, the tiny Iranian Anglican Diocese found almost all its leadership, lay and clerical, Iranian and expatriate, in prison. The Primate of the Province, himself in exile from Iran, appealed to the Archbishop of Canterbury to see what influence I could exert on behalf of his imprisoned clergy and laity. This was Terry's first involvement in such matters. When a Christian leader is asked to support and help his fellow Christians in such need there can only be one answer. Members of the church in South Africa and Namibia know how much he did to draw attention to the iniquities suffered by church people and church leaders there. But, with his success, further requests were difficult to refuse. Yet Terry's work has always been built on a Christian and humanitarian basis, and not a personal or political foundation. So the original request for help with hostages in Lebanon came through ECUSA from the Presbyterian Church of the USA on behalf of the Revd Benjamin Weir. Many of you will know Terry personally and will be eager to own him as a friend to our whole Communion. We pray for him and his wife and children – and that he will soon be safely returned to us.

I will not try to anticipate the details of our agenda. But in reading the many papers we have all been sent – actually I wouldn't claim to have mastered them all – I have been struck by the underlying quest for a clearer definition of the identity and vocation of the Anglican Communion. As you work through the many issues of Mission and Ministry, Dogmatic and Pastoral affairs, Ecumenical Relations, and Christianity and the Social Order, I shall be very surprised indeed if you are not confronted with basic questions about being an Anglican today.

The questions posed by the ordination of women to the priesthood and episcopate immediately raise the issue of authority in a divided Christianity. The relation between Christianity and culture sharply focuses the question of what it is which binds us together as an Anglican family. Ecumenical discussion about the goal of unity cannot be separated from questions about the future of Anglicanism: is the Communion a permanent or a provisional expression of Christianity? And questions of personal or social ethics return us to the problem of authority. In spite of the burden of paper and our apparently disparate agenda there is a deep inter-relatedness about our discussions of which we shall do well to be aware.

This has been illustrated for me already within the work of the Standing Committee in our discussion of the short but important document 'Centres of Authority in the Anglican Communion'. The working group which has produced this for us – under Archbishop Robin Eames of Armagh – was originally charged with the seemingly prosaic, not to say boring, task of reporting on the possibility of the creation of an inter-Anglican budget which would encompass the Lambeth Conference and the Primates' Meeting as well as this Council. From such unpromising ground the group rightly went on to pose some very important questions about being an Anglican which I hope you will all examine and ponder. As the report itself puts it:

> Any discussion of the relationship of bodies within the Communion involves a consideration of the nature of Anglicanism itself. It is not possible to divorce analysis of internal structures from what we have accepted as the overall ethos of Anglicanism. Nor is it possible to discuss structures without any awareness of and sensitivity to the ecumenical discussion of our experience.

We shall inevitably be faced with questions about centres of authority in the Communion because we meet only 15 months away from the Lambeth Conference. Our agenda will largely match theirs. All members of the Council will for the first time be present at the Conference. In the next two weeks we shall in effect be working at the relationship between the ACC and the Lambeth Conference. We need to have our eyes open for the *particular* contribution of a representative Council of Bishops, clergy and laity to the centres of authority of the Communion – just as the Bishops at Lambeth must look to their episcopal role and the task of 'bringing their dioceses with them'.

Perhaps the most difficult thing for me to master at this meeting will be the meal-coupon system! At the bottom in the small print it is stated that the coupon is non-exchangeable. There is in fact something gloriously non-exchangeable about a meeting of this Council. It is a unique gathering of Christians from all over the world in many different walks of life and with different roles within the Church. There is nothing like it. And, as we debate, deliberate and share meals together, I am quite content that the experience is non-exchangeable.

I will let another Archbishop have the last word – the Archbishop of Burma who for technical reasons cannot be at this meeting. He greets you all and writes of his deep regret at being unable to come from Burma to Singapore. He wishes us both a joyous and fruitful meeting and asks for someone to visit Burma afterwards so that they can share in our proceedings. I welcome you today in Archbishop Gregory's hope for a joyous and fruitful time together.

Left to right: the Secretary General (the Revd Canon Samuel Van Culin), the President (the Most Revd and Rt Hon. Robert Runcie) and the Chairman (the Venerable Yong Ping Chung)

Chairman's Address

Address given by the Venerable Yong Ping Chung, Chairman of the Anglican Consultative Council at the Opening Session of the Council, Sunday 26 April.

WELCOME TO SINGAPORE

May I welcome the President and all of you to Singapore. I am extremely pleased that my first meeting as Chairman of the ACC is held on my home ground. I would like to take this opportunity to express my gratitude to my Bishop, Bishop Luke Chhoa, who was already welcomed by the President earlier. I am grateful for all his encouragement and support to make my work as Chairman of the ACC possible. His reaction to my election as ACC Chairman was most encouraging. He said to me: 'You go ahead, Sabah is a small diocese. Your work in the ACC is our contribution to the world-wide Anglican Communion'. Bishop Chhoa is also Chairman of the Council of the Churches of East Asia and therefore considered as Primate of this part of the Anglican Communion.

My wife is with me today. A few of the wives are sitting in the Plenary Hall here. I like to take this opportunity to thank my wife and all the wives and spouses of our members who make our attendance at the ACC possible.

Since I became Chairman I have been very grateful for the support I have received from many people. Before Christmas I was invited to visit New Zealand. On my way home I was able to spend some time with our previous Chairman, John Denton. On your behalf I would like to send a message of greeting to John from this meeting.

In my first year as Chairman a person who helped me a great deal was Bishop Alastair Haggart, then Primus of the Scottish Episcopal Church. It was very helpful to have an experienced Vice-Chairman to assist me and to have my Vice-Chairman in the United Kingdom and in a position to be in regular contact with the Secretariat. I would also like to send a message to Bishop Haggart on your behalf. Bishop Haggart retired at the end of 1985, a great loss to me and the Standing Committee. But the Standing Committee elected Canon Colin Craston to serve as Vice-Chairman until this meeting. Canon Craston has proved to be a very good replacement. He has continued to be a very valuable point of contact between myself and the Secretariat and I am very grateful for all he has done. It is my hope that this meeting will elect Canon Craston to be our Vice-Chairman. Thus he will continue to help me through my term of office until ACC-8, and to see a new Chairman in until ACC-9.

ONE FAMILY

We come from many different countries and cultures but we are one family. We are bound together by 'Bonds of Affection' and one important part of our life together is our daily worship throughout this meeting.

Our family has many different languages. May I take this opportunity to remind you that for many of us English is not our first language and we have to translate mentally all we hear and say. Please remember this, and try to make your language simple and speak slowly. The last meeting of the Council asked that the Secretariat investigate having simultaneous translation at this meeting. All members were asked if they would require translation facilities. Everyone has said that they can manage to work in English but this does not mean that everyone is confident in English so I ask you all to be considerate to each other.

As members of this Council you have responsibilities both as representing your Churches to the Council and also in representing the Council to your Churches. The end of this meeting is not the end of your role as members of the Council. It is important that all members work at home to ensure that the report of the Council is fully used in their Province. Following ACC-6 Bishop Gitari, through the Kenyan Provincial Board of Education, carried out a very thorough study of 'Bonds of Affection'. If you would like to have a copy of the report, as an example of how one Province has dealt with the ACC report, please ask Deirdre Hoban for a copy.

MEETINGS OF THE STANDING COMMITTEE AND COUNCIL

Since ACC-6 your Standing Committee has had two meetings. In 1984 we met in Dunblane in Scotland and last year we met in Canada, immediately after the Primates' Meeting. We have now had a two day meeting here and hope that if we have to meet during the Council Meeting it will only be briefly. We have spoken about future meetings. We plan that the next meeting of the Standing Committee will be after the Lambeth Conference, in November 1988, back-to-back with the first meeting of the new Mission Issues and Strategy Advisory Group (MISAG-2). In 1989 we will meet in the Middle East, back-to-back with the Primates' Meeting. The next meeting of the Council will be in Wales and the proposed dates are July/August 1990. For ACC-9 we have been invited to Southern Africa. The Standing Committee realises that this may not be practical at that time but has taken the decision that the next time the Council meets in Africa it should be in South Africa and that the Council should meet there as soon as it is possible. An alternative site for ACC-9 is being investigated in Central America. Ireland has extended an invitation for ACC-10. The Standing Committee will discuss these sites at their meeting in 1988 so at present this is for your information.

One action the Standing Committee has taken which I want to report to you at once is to reappoint the Secretary General. Canon Van Culin's original appointment in 1983 was for five years with the hope that he would be appointed for a further five years. The Standing Committee was unanimous in agreeing to re-appoint him and I would like to take this opportunity to thank him for all he has done over the last five years and for his great contribution to the life of our Anglican family.

Canon Van Culin would say himself that he could not operate without his staff. There has been an increase in the number of staff at the Secretariat since our last meeting. The total number is now 17. This increase is partly due to the work being caused by the Lambeth Conference. I would like to take this opportunity to record our gratitude to the Church Commissioners for England who have seconded David Long to work at the ACC Secretariat as Deputy Secretary to the Lambeth Conference. He has been at the Secretariat since the beginning of this year and is with us here in Singapore.

We owe a great deal to all the ACC staff and we must acknowledge and thank them for the amount of work they are carrying. A number of them are here but there are also seven people still in London continuing the work of the Secretariat there. The Standing Committee has sent them a message of appreciation.

The members of the Standing Committee have each undertaken certain responsibilities during this meeting:

Worship – Bishop Joseph Iida
Finance sub Committee – Canon Colin Craston
Agenda Matters – Mrs Patricia Bays
Press and Media – Archbishop Robin Eames
Resolutions – Canon Winston Ndungane
Members concerns – Canon Benezeri Kisembo
Nominations Committee – Archbishop George Browne

INTER-ANGLICAN INFORMATION NETWORK

You have among your papers a brief report from John Martin about progress on the Inter-Anglican Information Network (known in the Secretariat as IAIN). If everything went according to plan it should be possible for the word processors in the office here to communicate directly with the word processors back in the ACC office. For example, it should be possible to have the final report of this Meeting transferred to London through a modem (a telephone line between two terminals) so that it can be accessed immediately in London. We hope that shortly there will be a computer link-up between London, New York, Nairobi and South Africa. The Secretary General will be able to give you more information about this project but at this point I feel we must record our thanks to Trinity Church in New York for their considerable help and support for IAIN.

NETWORKS

IAIN is one of about 17 Networks which the ACC is involved in at present. Two of them – Peace and Justice and the Family and Community Networks – have been meeting this last week and their input to the Christianity and Social Order Section will be important. I am glad that both Chairpeople of the Networks will be with us throughout this meeting. Faga Matalavea has chaired the Family and Community meeting and Charles Cesaretti, who is to serve as a Consultant to the Christianity and Social Order Section has been Convenor of the Peace and Justice Network for some years. We are particularly grateful to the Mission of St James and St John in Melbourne, and to the diocese of Melbourne, for enabling Alan Nichols and his colleagues to put such excellent work into the Family Project and we are pleased to have Alan with us again as Secretary to the Christianity and Social Order Section.

The ACC depends a great deal on the willingness of people to help us in many different areas of our work. I would like to introduce to you now the Section Secretaries who are giving us their time out of heavy workloads. Alan Nichols I have already mentioned. He is now Archdeacon of Melbourne. Another Australian, Bishop Kenneth Mason, Chairman of the Australian Board of Missions, is working with the Mission and Ministry Section. Richard Harries is at present Dean of King's College, London. He should have been with us in Nigeria but unfortunately was not able to attend that meeting. We are particularly grateful to him for giving time to us now to work on the Dogmatic and Pastoral Section as he is to be consecrated Bishop of Oxford on Ascension Day. Finally, we are glad to have Christopher Hill with us again as Secretary to the Ecumenical Section. As most of you know, he is Ecumenical Secretary to the Archbishop of Canterbury and Anglican Co-Secretary to the Anglican/Roman Catholic International Commission (ARCIC II).

9

INTER-ANGLICAN THEOLOGICAL AND DOCTRINAL COMMISSION

Since the last meeting of the Council the Report of the Inter-Anglican Theological and Doctrinal Commission has been published and you should all have received a copy of *For the Sake of the Kingdom*. The Standing Committee has decided to defer the appointment of a new Commission and the choice of a new subject until after the Lambeth Conference as they believe suitable subjects may become clear at that time.

MISSION ISSUES AND STRATEGY ADVISORY GROUP

The reconstitution of MISAG has to take place at this meeting. The Mission Agencies, at their Conference in Brisbane, selected their representatives, and the Standing Committee has agreed to ask the following Provinces to nominate members:

> Australia
> Brazil
> East Asia
> Kenya
> Nigeria
> USA

The Terms of Reference for MISAG-2 have still to be drawn up and the Standing Committee has referred this to the Mission and Ministry Section.

INTERNATIONAL CONFERENCE OF YOUNG ANGLICANS

ACC-6 proposed the setting up of a Youth Communication Network. Since ACC-6 the enthusiastic response from Provinces has resulted in a Conference for Young Anglicans being organised in Belfast, Northern Ireland, in January 1988. The Conference will be reflecting on the same themes as the Lambeth Conference and it is hoped that 350 young people will participate, including a significant ecumenical participation. The planning group for the Conference is aware that the Conference is a much bigger undertaking than was envisaged by ACC-6 and would welcome the endorsement of this Council. Lorna Helen, our youth member from Ireland, will be able to answer any questions about the Conference, and so will Deirdre Hoban, who is a member of the international planning group.

REVIEW OF THE ANGLICAN CENTRE IN ROME

ACC-6 asked that there should be a review of the work of the Anglican Centre in Rome. The Report of the Review Committee is included in your papers. It will be dealt with specifically by the Ecumenical Section but I hope that you have all had an opportunity to study it thoroughly. We are grateful to the Review Committee for the work they have done, and particularly to Professor Henry Chadwick who chaired the Committee and wrote the final report.

OFFICE RELOCATION

At ACC-6 it was assumed that by the time of this meeting the Secretariat would have moved to another location. For various reasons this move has been delayed and the Secretariat and their legal advisers are continuing negotiations about relocation.

UNITED NATIONS

Since the last meeting of the Council the ACC has received NGO (Non-Governmental Organization) affiliation with the United Nations. The Episcopal Church, USA, has drafted a job description for a staff person to implement this and has offered to make office space available in the Episcopal Church Center in New York and to provide the funds required for the position for the three years 1988 – 1990. The Standing Committee is extremely grateful to the Episcopal Church for this very generous offer.

LAMBETH CONFERENCE

All of you, in your Sections, will be discussing matters which relate to the Lambeth Conference. Canon Craston has written a paper on the role of ACC members at the Lambeth Conference which is to be distributed. I hope that each Section will take an opportunity to discuss this paper so that we all have an idea of what is expected of us as ACC members at the Lambeth Conference.

Finally let me say that I look forward to working with you all during this meeting. We pray for the success of this meeting and for its deliberations.

Many Gifts, One Spirit

Archbishop of Canterbury's Sermon

The following is the text of the sermon preached by the Archbishop of Canterbury at St Andrew's Cathedral, Coleman Street, Singapore, on Sunday, 26 April 1987, at the opening of the seventh meeting of the Anglican Consultative Council.

Christ is Risen – He is Risen Indeed. Grace and Peace to you through God our Father and the Lord Jesus Christ. I bring to the Christian people of Singapore an Easter greeting of love and gratitude for your vibrant faith, and for your generous hospitality towards all of us who have journeyed here.

Personally, I am mindful of St Paul's words 'I thank my God each time I remember you'. On previous visits I have experienced and recognized the movement of the Spirit here and the growth of the Church. It is no bad thing for the representatives of the Anglican Communion to be travelling at Easter. Let our time here be a kind of *pilgrimage*. The pilgrimage in any religious tradition calls for three things – a cause, companionship and memories to take away. Last Monday our Cathedral at Canterbury was filled with thousands of young people – some from your countries but most from mine. No observer could doubt the cause – the singing, the banners, the slogans all conveyed the assurance of Christ's Resurrection and the desire to offer to him for his blessing and direction the varying ideals and enthusiasms of youth – peace, feeding the hungry, housing the homeless. They were a mixed lot by old-fashioned labels of church allegiance; and the best thing you see on pilgrimage is the way in which children, handicapped, strangers, seekers after faith, the lonely or shy, are drawn in and made to feel part of it.

This companionship had its most memorable moment when each pilgrim raised his lighted candle during the reading of the Easter Gospel and, looking over them, individuals seemed to merge in one bright light. There was a unity in Christ deeper than the opinions which divided us. So a powerful memory was taken away of the light of the Risen Christ, and a determination to carry it into the shadows of our days of trouble and to spread it in the dark places of the world.

May these two weeks be something of an Easter pilgrimage for us in which we renew our confidence in the cause we all share. May we draw strength from keeping company with so many of our fellow believers from whom we are often separated by distance and by opinions. And, at the end, may our memories be an inspiration which will renew and strengthen our brothers and sisters in the places where Christ has called us to serve him.

The Scriptures all convey a sense of movement and discovery in the story of Holy Week and Easter. After Good Friday the followers of Jesus were demoralized and scattered. Like us they made journeys. Some went back to Galilee. Others took the road to nearby Emmaus. The women went to the tomb outside the city walls. Only then did they experience the presence of the living Lord. Only then did they come together again in the Upper Room to receive the peace of the Risen Lord and the gift of the Holy Spirit for their renewal and for the foundation of the Christian Church.

We must honestly admit that as individuals and as the institutional Church we often fail to recognize the Risen Lord when he comes to meet us. Only in the breaking of the bread did the two disciples finally recognise who was with them on their journey to Emmaus. Mary Magdalene at first supposed the Lord to be the gardener. The eleven on the mountain in Galilee worshipped Jesus – but Matthew also tells us that 'some doubted'. In this Easter week of the Risen Lord I want to talk to you about recognizing the Resurrection when we see it – as individuals, as the Church here in Singapore, and as the gathered representatives of the Anglican Communion.

The first step to recognizing the Resurrection is to cease to locate it exclusively in the remote past or the distant future – where Resurrection can be safely tamed as an historical fact or a future dream without immediate relevance to living experience today. So our theological debates about the first Easter or about our ultimate destiny can actually be a distraction from the Resurrection now. In St John's Gospel, at the raising of Lazarus, Martha says, quite correctly of course, 'I know we will rise again in the Resurrection at the last day'. But Jesus said to her: 'I *am* the Resurrection and the life'. Resurrection is present tense. Just as the psalmist in tonight's psalm warns us about identifying the present and living God with cult-idols, so we must never reduce Resurrection to the distant past or the speculative future. 'I *am* the Resurrection and the life', says the Lord.

Even if we look to the present for Resurrection, there is still the danger of mistaking the image for the real thing. There's a tendency to identify the revolutionary experience of the living Christ with the day-to-day compromises of the Church. Our personal piety and spirituality, our ecclesiastical organizations, our businesslike bureaucracy can all be used to shield us from what an Anglican monk once called 'the threatening glory of resurrection'. He went on like this:

> If as Christians we are supposed to believe Christ *is* the resurrection, it is strange that life for us invariably means business as usual ... the preservation of the status quo ... provided that, in each case, there is a respectable measure of reform: in the individual mostly moral, and in the Church mostly administrative.

The problem is a fatal tendency to cover up the Cross. **We** beautify it, we decorate it, we exalt it. We do anything but recognize it as an instrument of death. We go to any lengths to avoid signs of death in ourselves and in the Church.

The Cross is a bitter reminder to us of the compromises, failures, and evasions of our personal life. We sometimes even use our pieties for protection against a hard world. The Cross also often seems a long way from the institutions of the Church. We defend our ecclesiastical empires, we build up our international institutions. We become nervous when prophets speak of needing to die so that there may be new life.

So we must first learn the hard and bitter lesson of Good Friday. Good Friday comes whether we like it or not. We cannot avoid the personal and institutional crosses we have to carry. What we can do is to beg for the strength to accept them as God's will and as occasions for Resurrection and real renewal. That which I find most difficult to face in myself, that which I least want to recognize in the Church, is also the place where life after death is truly found.

Our travelling at Eastertide gives us the opportunity to discover the miracle of Resurrection within the ordinary round and daily routine of our lives. Resurrection happens to us as we are – as individuals and as the Church – and its coming is usually quiet and unobtrusive. Sometimes it is only later that we recognize that we have been raised to newness of life. I hope that this Eastertide meeting of the Anglican Consultative Council here in Singapore will be a time for such recognition in all of us. As we meet here with the local Church of Singapore and, as the members of the Council debate the matters in its large agenda, I hope we shall have our eyes open for the miracle of Resurrection.

The Council, on doctrine, will be faced with difficult questions raised by the uniqueness of Christ and the living presence of the other great faiths of the world. My visit to India this time last year brought this home to me powerfully. Shall we have the courage to recognize others along the journey of spiritual pilgrimage? Shall we be able to glimpse something of the Eternal Word who comes to enlighten every man? Or shall we fight for the exclusive possession of the light of Christ by Christians?

Some of us need to ask whether we have confined the Risen Christ and seen him only in Western cultural dress. We need to recognize those to whom the Risen Christ speaks and makes himself known in the tones and forms of Asia. We shall need to consider the relation of the eternal, incarnate and Risen Lord to all human endeavour.

14

We live in a world where agonizing decisions have to be made if what is now scientifically possible is to serve truly human values. New techniques in embryology face men and women of all faiths and none with new and difficult ethical questions. How do we recognize the Risen Christ in the medical scientist or the infertile couple who long for God's gift of children? But alongside new scientific possibilities there are also new and terrible diseases. How do we uphold standards of biblical chastity and fidelity and also proclaim the Gospel of God's suffering love to the young person dying of AIDS? And there is the age-old problem of hunger and the new debate about development. How do we proclaim Christ as the living Bread to the child dying of malnutrition?

We shall be talking about unity. How do we proclaim the Gospel of reconciliation to all nations in a world divided into North and South, East and West, by poverty or politics, while the Christian Churches remain themselves divided and we Anglicans squabble over the ordination of women?

These are some of the questions the ACC will be facing. Here is where we look for resurrection and renewal.

For the Diocese of Singapore, our generous and joyous hosts today and in the coming weeks, there will be similar Eastertide reflections. Our second lesson tonight reminds us of the many gifts of the Spirit which are needed for building up the body of Christ. There is so much to be thankful for in the renewed life of the Church here. But we must always be ready to recognize all God's gifts in all God's people. It was said long ago 'There is no stopping place in this life. No, nor was there ever one no matter how far along the way we've come. This then above all things: be ready for the gifts of God and always for new ones.'

St Paul's letter to the Christians at Corinth calls us to recognize the gifts God had given to *others* as well as ourselves. So today we joyfully recognize the gifts of other Christians of different traditions who join us in these two weeks. We shall also remember that Singapore is the home of the Christian Conference of Asia. We shall remember that Anglicans never claim to be more than *part* of the one Holy Catholic Church throughout the world. Our vocation will always be defined in ecumenical terms. And here in Asia we cannot but be reminded of the gifts of the poor – in which we must also recognize the face of the dying and Risen Christ.

Those of us who live in countries where the standard of living of the majority rises year by year need to listen to the voices of those 'left behind'. It may be the urban unemployed or immigrant communities. In Singapore

15

we can also recognize the gifts which minority groups such as the Filipinos have to bring to the Church and the wider community.

So I pray our meeting here in Singapore will be an opportunity for renewal. I hope that here the Churches of the Anglican Communion may learn to make the new life of God's kingdom more readily accessible. Let Singapore be a place where we recognize Resurrection, we celebrate it, share it, and carry its inspiration away with with us to our homes.

I will end by giving you an illustration of the Church I want to see.

Some of you will know the book or the film *A Room with a View*. It's the story of a young English girl's awakening on a first visit to Italy. On her return to England Lucy's neatly ordered life is thrown off balance. The conventional relationship with her family and fiancé are threatened by the spontaneous promptings of her heart for George, the man she comes to love in spite of the divisions of class and social background.

There are two Anglican clergymen in E. M. Forster's novel – and for me they are parables of two kinds of Church. There is the Chaplain in Florence, the Reverend Cuthbert Eager: a consummate snob and puritan who despises George because his family are in Florence 'for trade'. Then there is Mr Beebe, of whom Lucy says 'He seems to see good in everyone. No-one would take him for a clergyman'. It is Mr Beebe who instinctively sees that Lucy must break out of the conventional patterns of life which surround and entomb her. In Italy this does not quite happen, but Mr Beebe knows it will happen one day. He has noticed how passionately Lucy plays the piano and says this of her:

'Does it seem reasonable that she should play so wonderfully, and live so quietly? I suspect that one day she will be wonderful in both. The watertight compartments in her will break down, and music and life will mingle.'

Let Mr Beebe be our model for the Church. A Church which allows life and music to mingle. A Church which encourages renewal, awakening and resurrection. Mr Beebe concludes his conversation by saying of Lucy:

'There was simply the sense that she had found her wings and meant to use them.'

To this I would add the last verses of today's psalm:

The dead do not praise the Lord: nor do any that go down to silence. But *we* will bless the Lord: both now and for evermore. O praise the Lord.

May we discover this together in Singapore through our journeyings and our meetings, and may we bless the Lord among the living now and ever-more.

May we too find our wings – and intend to use them, to the greater glory of God – Father, Son and Holy Spirit. Amen.

Left to right: The Archbishop of Canterbury, the Chairman and the Rt Revd Moses Tay, Bishop of Singapore.

Review Address: A Family Gathering

Review Address given Monday, 27 April, by the Revd Canon Samuel Van Culin, Secretary General of the Anglican Consultative Council at the Seventh Meeting of the Council – ACC-7: Singapore 1987.

ACC STAFF

One of the pleasures of a family gathering is that it gives you the opportunity to talk about yourself – not only as an individual but as a family. This family gathering of the ACC is no exception. The Archbishop of Canterbury has introduced new members of this ACC family who have come to this gathering from a large number of the member Churches. I have the pleasure of introducing four individuals who serve on the staff of this family and who have joined us in the three years since we last gathered in Badagry, Nigeria.

We have a new colleague on our staff responsible for communication and publishing. Mr Robert Byers comes to us from the Church of Ireland. He succeeded Mr John Martin from the Church in Australia who was our first Communication Officer and is now concentrating on editorial work and consultancy in communication and publishing. John Martin continues to assist us in special projects – most especially in the development of the Inter-Anglican Information Network (IAIN). Bob Byers has developed our press and media links since his arrival two years ago, expanded our Communication Network, initiated careful planning for media at the Lambeth Conference in 1988, and played a key role in the development of our Inter-Anglican Publishing Network. This publishing network includes, at present eleven Provinces of the Anglican Communion which now, for the first time, are capable of publishing books and other material in eleven different Provinces simultaneously. Printing takes place in six Provinces. This is a tremendous step forward and it has been accompanied by the initiation of a capacity to publish in different languages – presently in French, Portuguese, Japanese and Spanish. As these initiatives and skills grow and develop, the family strengthens its ability to communicate effectively.

The Revd Canon Martin Mbwana is responsible for Mission and Social Concerns. He joined us from the Church in Tanzania where he served as Provincial Officer for nine years and where he was Chancellor of the Diocese of Zanzibar and Tanga. Martin and his wife Jane and their six daughters have now spent two cold winters with us in London. Their survival is a tremendous encouragement to us all! He has resuscitated the Partners in Mission Consultation process and helped to bring the Communion-wide Conference of Anglican Mission Agencies to a happy conclusion.

You have their report in your papers for this meeting. Anglican Mission Agencies represent one of the many important and growing networks that are developing in the communion. There are, at present, sixteen networks at one phase or another of development. It is Martin Mbwana's responsibility to oversee and relate to the majority of them. Prior to the gathering here in Singapore of the ACC we had almost 25 people working hard for four days in the Family and Community Study Network and an equal number in the Peace and Justice Network. You will have the results on their work at this meeting. Martin's report on networks which will be within your papers is a very important and brief analysis of who they are, how important they are, and the things we must consider as we try to nourish and sustain them within the family.

Mr David Long has joined us as deputy secretary for the Lambeth Conference, 1988. He is a senior staff officer of the Church Commissioners for England and has been fully seconded to us by the Commissioners for 1987 and 1988 to carry the load of detailed planning and arrangements for the next Lambeth Conference. He is involving himself in every aspect of the work of the Secretariat because the ACC, the Primates' Meeting and the Lambeth Conference are so deeply inter-related. His addition to our staff has brought relief and encouragement to all and he is inexhaustible in his attention to every detail that will assure the Archbishop of Canterbury that he and all concerned can have confidence in the management of the next Lambeth Conference.

Bishop Michael Nazir-Ali has joined us as assistant to the Archbishop of Canterbury for co-ordinating Studies for the Lambeth Conference. He was, until recently, Bishop of Raiwind in the Church of Pakistan. He is at present Director to the Centre for Mission Studies in Oxford. He is responsible for assisting the Church to engage in the study of the themes related to the next Lambeth Conference. He is here at this gathering of the ACC because of the important contribution that is made by the ACC to the development of the study of these themes in the Churches of the Communion. He has a major responsibility for the St Augustine's Seminar that will be meeting this July/August. We are fortunate to have a man of such training and experience carrying this responsibility for Lambeth studies.

These four colleagues join with thirteen others who make the full complement of seventeen people who run and sustain the office of this Anglican family located in London. The Secretariat serves the ACC, the Meeting of Primates, the Lambeth Conference, and the Inter-Anglican Networks that are in place and emerging. There is a spirit of dedication and caring within the staff that goes well beyond the limits of duty and job description. I take this opportunity to salute and thank them all.

AN ASIAN CONTEXT

This meeting of the Anglican Consultative Council, its seventh in succession, is the first to be held East of Suez. The Council has met twice on the African Continent, once in the West Indies, once in Canada, once in Ireland and once in England.

Our meeting here in Singapore gives us the opportunity to take note of the life and witness of the Churches in Asia and the Pacific. They live here within the great cultural traditions that stretch across this enormous geographical space of continents and islands. For Anglicans there are seven Provinces and Councils in this region including Australia, Burma, the Council of East Asia, Japan, Melanesia, New Zealand, and Papua New Guinea. There are also the two Dioceses of the Church of Sri Lanka which, like the Dioceses in the Church in Korea and Malaysia and here in Singapore, are under the Metropolitical oversight of the Archbishop of Canterbury. Within this region there are seventy Anglican Dioceses. Anglicans, here, worship in numerous languages, including Chinese, English, Japanese, Korean, Melanesian, Maori, Malay, Arabic, Singhalese, Igorote and Burmese.

Here, in Asia, ecumenical initiatives of far reaching importance have been undertaken – certainly initiatives that have had very deep impact on the life of the Churches of the Anglican Communion. Anglicans entered the united Church of North India, the Church of South India, and the Church of Pakistan as founding members. The Churches of the Anglican Communion are in full Communion with these Churches and the representatives of these Churches sit as members of this Anglican Consultative Council even as Bishops from these Churches and from the Church of Bangladesh will be attending the forthcoming Lambeth Conference in 1988. In addition Anglican Churches are in full Communion with the Mar Thoma Syrian Church of Malabar and with the Philippine Independent Church, both of which Churches are represented at meetings of the ACC. Bishops of these Churches are invited to the forthcoming Lambeth Conference. We celebrate these relationships and we rejoice in them. In them we can recognize the emergence of a Communion of episcopal Churches which share a common faith, the sacraments, and the historic threefold ministry. We need to recognize and support those former Anglican brethren who have taken the important and hopeful step into full ecclesial union in these United Churches. The voice of these Churches must continue to be heard in Anglican gatherings and discussions. They have a special contribution to make in ecumenical dialogue and we should make a concerted effort, I believe, to explore ways in which they can be more adequately represented in Anglican discussions with other Christian Churches.

CHRISTIANITY AND CULTURE

Our meeting here in Asia can serve to remind us that mission exists within culture. By culture, in this instance, I mean all that human beings do together to develop and sustain their shared life in Community – their language, their creation myths, their kingship and kinship systems, their religious practices, their arts and artefacts. A human being does not enter life unless he or she enters at least one of these living cultures. If they are to know God's love for themselves, then God's love must find them *there*, where God first placed them. God's love enters each life through a distinct and special door. This fact affects decisively the mission of the Church and this fact affects the building of communion between Churches. This truth is at the heart of the report from the Inter-Anglican Theological and Doctrinal Commission, *For the Sake of the Kingdom,* which we are receiving official-ly at this meeting of the Council and which is a study document for the Lambeth Conference 1988.

Christianity is not a recent colonial import into Asia. It appeared in the heartlands of Asia as early as the sixth century AD. The Anaradjapura Cross – a Nestorian Cross set on a lotus – found carved in a pillar which once held up the roof of a shopkeeper in Anaradjapura, North Ceylon, testifies to the existence of a Christian community before the fifth century. The Bishop of Kurunagala, here at the ACC, wears one. On the Sian-fu tablet in China we find an eighth century summary of Christian doctrine and a review of Chinese church history. Carved above this inscription is again a cross set on the lotus (a typical Buddhist symbol) while issuing from under it are clouds – often associated in popular Taoism with the sages. Christ, the true sage sits on the throne of Buddha! There are examples of Persian crosses going back to around the ninth century in the art of the Syrian Christians on the Malabar coast in India. Here in this Asian context Christianity has met and lived with the most important, developed, and sophisticated ancient religious and religious/cultural systems. In Buddhism, Hinduism and Confucianism there are in Asia strong, historic and cul-turally coherent religious traditions which dominate and pervade in one way or another all of the peoples of Asia and many of the peoples of the Pacific.

INTER-FAITH RELATIONSHIPS

Inter-faith relationships have been the subject of discussions at the last three meetings of this Council. In nearly every Province of the Communion Anglicans live in close proximity with followers of other religions. For many of our Provinces inter-faith encounter has only just begun but there are many others where it has been a fact of daily life for centuries. Here in Asia we are reminded of that dramatically.

The Churches of Asia are experiencing what Churches elsewhere in the world are experiencing – the fact that societies everywhere are moving towards greater openness and pluralism. In spite of isolated examples to the contrary – for example, Iran – there is no doubt that this is increasingly and powerfully true. Even the monolithic socialist societies cannot resist this current. In many cases, the emergence of a plural society makes the existence of Christian Churches, in a predominantly non-Christian culture, possible. In others, societies which have hitherto been largely Christian become increasingly plural with many different old and new faiths represented in them.

ANGLICAN DECISION MAKING

This increasing pluralism and openness in society is reflected in the life of the Church. Most of the important issues confronting the Church today reflect this. Our efforts in the Anglican Communion, as an example, to describe our common faith in Christ in words and images that speak to and touch the contemporary human experience, reflect this. The Bishop of Durham helps many who hear him – but not all. Our initiatives to reform liturgy in order to embrace more adequately the whole people of God in their offering of life and prayer reflect this. Our efforts to find a full place for women in the full ministry of the Church reflect this. And our continued commitment to search for a communion of Churches that can live in a state of ordered freedom reflects this. The Inter-Anglican Theological and Doctrinal Commission has reminded us that 'we have argued that pluralism can serve the cause of a deeper and fuller understanding of the Gospel and so of a deeper and fuller unity in Christ'.

This is not a time in which we can expect a common set of practices, everywhere, uniform throughout the Church. It is, rather a time when, following the lead of the Doctrinal Commission, we can assert the positive values of comprehensiveness within the Communion. It is a time when Anglicans can affirm the positive value of holding a variety of practices together in a communion of Churches.

You will be hearing of the work of a small study group which has been meeting this year in your name to examine some of the implications for our family of the nature of Anglicanism as it appears to be emerging at this time. This group has something to say to us about the inter-relationship of the ACC and the Lambeth Conference, the Primates and the See of Canterbury. Above all else, they are asking us questions about how we can as a family make decisions.

We are often asked how do Anglicans make decisions? This is an important question both in our ecumenical relationships and in our life within the Communion! As we face the question of the ordination of women to the priesthood and to the episcopate, as we face the meaning and character of renewal in the Church, as we seek to articulate the nature of moral life for a Christian facing the changes in family life, human sexuality, and genetic engineering, and as we try to live out and understand the very nature of the communion we have with each other we must understand how Anglicans make decisions. I would answer – 'We make decisions in a way similar to that of the early Church'. In his excellent little book *Decision Making in the Church – a Biblical Model* Professor Luke T. Johnson analyses examples of decision-making in the early Church. He explores especially the decisions the early Church had to make about the conversion of Cornelius and his baptism by Peter. What Johnson describes about decision-making in the early Church can be applied with validity to the nature of decision-making in the Church in the fourth century on the Doctrine of the Trinity, to the church in the fifteenth and sixteenth centuries on the issue of the Reformation, and to the Church in the twentieth century on the vocation to unity and the commitment to the Ecumenical Movement. He makes the following observation:

> The decision is not made all at once. It is not made by the entire Church from the beginning. It is not made on the basis of *a priori* principles and practices. Even the scripture and the words of Jesus are re-read. The decision, rather, is the result of a long process, involving many believers in many places, and the decisions of many local communities. The experiences of diverse people and the narrative of those experiences – in an ever-widening circle – provide the primary theological data. As those who testify speak of their experience of God, so do those who listen and weigh what is said: they exercise discernment. The people who have these experiences, moreover, are people already attentive to the Lord in prayer, and thus open to the new and surprising ways God might act, both in their own and others' lives. *Slowly, the story of individuals becomes the narrative of the Church.*

This is the way the Church still makes decisions. We are living in a world in which all Churches are having to remember the fact that even so-called 'final decisions' can be, and are going to be, openly discussed and disputed. While Anglicans accept that there must be discipline, we also have a conviction that patience and toleration are essential in the discernment of God's will in the life of his Church. There has to be a willingness to see how new experiences and understandings commend themselves to the common heart and mind of the Church – often after prolonged debate and argument. While Anglicans have evolved consultative procedures at the international level – the ACC, the Primates' Meeting, and the Lambeth Conference especially – we are still a family of Churches that gives canonical power to

23

decision-making in the particular local context. This requires of us that we appreciate and indeed affirm the importance of local decision-making as a contribution to the developing life of the Church – as long as local decision-making is kept in healthy inter-action with the wider Church through consultation, and as long as local decision-making is constrained by the will and commitment of the local Church to maintain itself in the life of the wider Communion. We cannot and do not expect every Church in the Communion to grow and develop at the same pace or in the same manner. The nature and expression and exercise of ministry varies as does the quality of the Church's witness, its experience of renewal, its teaching on marriage and divorce, its presentation of liturgy, and its pastoral understanding and care for people in all sorts and conditions of life. Anglicans have made a decision to live with this variety and to learn from it because of our conviction of the importance of decision-making being held close to the local Church. It means, of course, that we have lived with a variety of local practices on many occasions in our life together as a Communion, even as we do today.

ANGLICAN CENTRES OF UNITY

But while we are a family of Churches that gives canonical power to decision-making in the particular local context, then we are, also, a family of Churches who have made a mutual commitment and agreement to consult with one another and who strive to preserve unity with each other. This is the work of the Anglican Consultative Council, the Meeting of the Primates, the Lambeth Conference and the Archbishop of Canterbury. The *Anglican Consultative Council* studies and discusses a wide range of matters confronting the various Churches at the local level and it assists the Churches in sustaining Networks for continuing planning and initiative across the world. When it shares the results of its consultations with the local Church, it is exercising its vocation to assist the Churches in fulfilling their mission and in preserving their unity with each other. When the *Primates* meet they assist each other in their witness and identify those tensions both within the Churches, and between the Churches that threaten to undermine their unity with each other. They thus return to their own Churches with a deeper understanding of the way in which the office of Primate can be exercised in the preservation of unity within the Church and between the Churches. When the *Lambeth Conference of Bishops* meets it speaks with the most authoritative voice within the life of the Communion. It is here that 'the mind of the Churches' within the Anglican Communion can be revealed most comprehensively. Lambeth speaks to the Church about its Unity and Mission and to the world about God's love for it in Christ. When *the Archbishop of Canterbury* speaks and acts as the centre of affection and as the pastoral office in whom all the Churches of the Communion meet each other, he exercises his vocation both to gather the church in council and to guide and assist the Church in witness, service, and in the preservation of its unity.

I have focused these remarks on Church and culture and on decision-making. I have done so because I believe that the ACC is a prototype of the wider Communion drawn out of many lands and cultures and living and witnessing in many different contexts. You bring these differences with you but you also bring out of your Churches and out of your Christian conviction your commitment to preserve and build up the unity of the Church and to support each other in the witness and service of the Church in its many parts. By your exercise of forbearance, charity and fraternal consultation, you are assisting your Churches and the wider Anglican Communion to make its decisions as a living community. What you do here must be faithful. But what you do back in your Churches following this consultation will be essential – to assist your bishops and synods to engage with each other on the major themes of the Lambeth Conference 1988 in such a way that you can help the bishops of your Church to 'bring their Dioceses with them'.

In his book *The Futures of Christianity* David L Edwards, Provost of Southwark, has written of the Anglican Communion that 'for the futures of Christianity, here is a small model which allows much diversity, theological and cultural, in order to welcome truth and reality, even at the price of being, or of appearing to be, untidy, confused and broken; and here is an experiment (often a failure) which is admirable precisely because, when at its best, it has never claimed to have reached all the answers'. Here is a description, appropriately modest, of a great vocation which lies before the Anglican Communion.

Every family, when it gathers, has those who talk too much. Perhaps I have done that. But, if so, accept it, please, as an expression of love for the family and of hope that the family will reflect the mind of Christ wherever we are dispersed in the world.

PART 2 – SECTION REPORTS
Section I – Mission and Ministry

A. MISSION

1. MISSION

(a)   The Report of the Anglican Consultative Council Meeting in Badagry, Nigeria, 1984 dealt very fully with Mission. The section on Mission (pp 46-61 *Bonds of Affection*), and indeed the whole report, is strongly commended to the Church. Commended as well is the report of the Mission Issues and Strategy Advisory Group (MISAG), *Giving Mission its Proper Place.*

(b)   This section identified as its main responsibility the following three subjects:

    i.   The Report *Progress in Partnership* of the Brisbane Mission Agencies Conference of December 1986.

    ii.   The Terms of Reference for MISAG-2 (see p. 34).

    iii.   A Statement about some aspects of Renewal in Mission.

2. PROGRESS IN PARTNERSHIP

(a)   A Conference was held in Brisbane, Australia from 8-13 December 1986 as the result of a decision made at ACC-6. (Resolution 12 ACC-6). The purpose of the conference was to assist Mission Agencies and the Churches of the Communion to have a better understanding of current mission issues, agency policies, practices and resources, with a view to a more faithful stewardship in God's mission today.

Three specific Mission Topics were considered by the Conference –

    i.   Assessing Evangelism as part of Mission

    ii.   Assessing Development as part of Mission

    iii.   Ecumenical Sharing in Mission

The Partners in Mission (PIM) process was examined under the following aspects:

    i.   The way in which the PIM process is lived out especially in terms of relationships, and

    ii.   The way in which present structures assist or inhibit mutuality in partnership in the Anglican Communion.

Two reports have been published. One is *Progress in Partnership* which includes the texts of the major addresses given at the Conference, and the
other *Equal Partners,* a more popular account compiled and written by
Archdeacon Alan Nichols of Melbourne.

(b)   The word 'agency' was used to describe the participants in an attempt
to recognise the diversity of the Anglican Communion. Some Provinces
have one Board or Department of Mission which is a part of its central administration while others, particularly England and Australia, have a
number of voluntary societies or boards. The decision to hold this conference partly came from the belief that the Anglican Communion could no
longer afford the luxury of diverse, and at times divergent, philosophies and
practices without some mutual understanding and commitment to co-
operation.

It was also noted that ACC-6 spoke of the imbalances that exist because of
the prevailing 'maintenance mentality' of many churches which hinders and
can prevent an effective proclamation of the Gospel and reaching out in service. The multiplicity of agencies with their different practices also makes
for imbalances in the use of resources and manpower. The Church cannot
be blind to those inequities which in the light of the Gospel are wrong, and
are within the bounds of its own initiatives to make more equable, whether
they are in the manner of its witness or of its sharing.

(c)   *Partners' Statement*

An important contribution was made at the conference by the representatives of those churches who have traditional links with the various missionary bodies of the Communion. As this Statement stands in its own right
in the report it is printed here in full:

i.   We believe this first Mission Agencies' Conference has been a rich experience
for all of us. We have grown in mutual knowledge and sharing. We appreciate the invitation to participate. We wish to express our thanks to the Chairman of the Conference for his sensitivity to us all, and to the Primate of Australia and the Australian
Church for their warm welcome and hospitality.

ii.   We have tried our best to participate by speaking and listening; but English is
not our first language and our participation was at times limited by this fact. There is
need for our partners to bear this in mind and avoid using unnecessary colloquial
language.

iii.   We were greatly encouraged by the spirit of understanding, the willingness of
Mission Agencies to listen to us and to one another, and their readiness to respond to
the changing demands of the mission of the Church.

iv.   We have always been unhappy with the unconscious 'first world' tendency to
tell us what is the best for us without 'taking us seriously'. In the language of Dermot
Dorgan's paper we also are 'donors'. We are willing to accept invitations to offer

what we can. II Corinthians 8:4-15 is the church model for our Communion. In this model all we have is to be shared; because we are one!

v. We commend the views expressed in the papers presented on the PIM process, which very much reflected the concerns of all of us.

vi. As representatives of 'third world' Provinces we realise that we do not know each other sufficiently. We need channels to enable us to build up mutual understanding and knowledge. We need to share experiences in order to get to know each other and to grow together. *We have therefore urged each other to take the following suggestions seriously:*

(a) Inter-Provincial communication and exchange of information.

(b) The organisation of conferences in each region following the example of the first Latin American Congress to be held in Panama in November 1987.

(c) A 'third world' Anglican Provinces PIM consultation so that we may share what we are.

(d) The establishment of a 'companion diocese programme' among the 'third world' Provinces.

vii. As for the Mission Agencies, while we recognise the need to work through them in mission, they need to improve their relationships with their Churches.

viii. We wish this Conference and any follow-up machinery every success and God's blessing.

Partnership implies that there will be continual communication and it is very necessary that isolated parts of the Communion are kept in touch with each other and that the Communion as a whole be ready to respond to particular needs. While the Partner Churches at this Conference would wish to be able to communicate better with one another, the lack is by no means confined to them. All too frequently neighbours are ignored or taken for granted.

(d) *Evangelism as part of Mission*

The Church in each place carries primary responsibility for evangelism in that place, although it may ask for assistance from elsewhere. There may be a need in certain circumstances for agencies of mission themselves to make suggestions or offers in the spirit of partnership. Being open to one another is difficult as churches assume more and more responsibility for their own lives; and agencies are often insensitive to this growth as well as appearing to be unrelated to the life of their own churches. Some donors claim the recipients of their gifts could not exist without them whereas the reverse might be the truth.

The reality of our times calls for a radical reappraisal of mission strategies if the Church is to adequately reckon with the changed context of mission in this religiously, culturally, racially, socially, ideologically pluralist society.

The challenge of this changed context for mission must be taken seriously so that appropriate responses and activities may be developed.

Attention of the churches and their agents in mission is drawn to such resource material as *Guidelines in Dialogue* (WCC 1979); *Towards a Theology for Inter-faith Dialogue* (ACC 1986); *My Neighbour's Faith and Mine – Theological Discoveries Through Interfaith Dialogue* (WCC 1986).

(e)   *Development as Part of Mission*

The ACC-6 Report has a large section on Social Transformation (*Bonds of Affection* pp 57-5.4). The Council felt this term more adequately described what is meant by the word development. *Progress in Partnership* reiterated the firm belief that human development is an integral part of mission and, while recognising the difficulty of holding all aspects of mission together, accepted the necessity of striving to resolve them so that social transformation could take place as people responded to the Gospel.

(f)   *Ecumenical Sharing*

Much more work needs to be done before genuine ecumenical thrust in mission happens. The churches must maintain their membership of ecumenical bodies rather than avoid or leave them. It is so easy to retreat into a safe haven and there stagnate rather than take the risk of co-operation, get a bit dirty and find the Lord together.

(g)   *Data Gathering*

Transparency and accountability were two words which figure largely in the Report of MISAG 1. It was agreed in Brisbane that the collecting, collating and analysing of facts and figures about the Anglican Communion would help the Church realise the ideals these words express. The purpose of the data-gathering would be to provide a centralised and computerised base of information so that the churches of the Anglican Communion, their departments, boards and societies of mission would have access to accurate information.

(h)   *Partners in Mission*

The conference looked carefully at the way the Communion had embraced Partnership in Mission. It agreed PIM is designed to create and sustain relationships, not just to promote a single or isolated consultations. The visitors who are the representatives at consultations of the Partner Churches are there as facilitators; people, who through their questions and comments will help the host church to recognise its opportunities, make best use of its resources and increase its faithfulness as well as accept its shortcomings.

Like any important event, the preparation for a consultation is absolutely vital. No partner church representative can ask the right questions without well-researched and well-presented data.

As Partnership in Mission is a process, so too is constant evaluation and appraisal of mission. Although the term 'mission audit' is not acceptable to some, the process it describes is vital. The Report of ACC-6, *Bonds of Affection* (Resolution 11 p 60) sets out in some detail information about a mission audit and it is strongly recommended to the church.

(i) *The Mission Agencies Working Group*

The Brisbane Conference set up a working group to carry forward the intention of the agencies to co-operate in such tasks as:

    i.   Co-ordinating agencies' responses to agreed PIM priorities;

    ii. Assisting the ACC in a system of data gathering;

    iii. Assisting the ACC draft guidelines for companion diocese relations;

    iv. Exploring the feasibility of establishing loan funds in various parts of the Communion;

    v.   Undertaking research on criteria for appropriate Development Programmes;

The agencies are very aware of the words from their partners about superiority, directiveness, insensitivity and the need for the agencies to help build up church-to-church relationships where presently there is an agency-church relationship. The working group will help agencies to be mutually supportive as they respond to these situations.

While this group is an arrangement made between the agencies, those agencies see it very much as a servant of the Communion using MISAG-2 as a body to which to respond and through which to report.

Resolution 1: Mission Agencies

THAT this Council:

(a)   receives the Report of the Mission Agencies Conference held in Brisbane, Australia, in December 1986 entitled *Progress in Partnership;* commends the conference on its work and refers the Report to the Standing Committee and to MISAG-2 for appraisal and appropriate action;

(b)   affirms the Partnership in Mission Programme, notes the statement printed below from the Mission Agencies Conference and refers it to the Standing Committee with comments;

31

(c)   welcomes the Mission Agencies' offer to engage in a feasibility study, in consultation with ACC, to determine the cost in money and human resources of an international-data bank and that this be referred to the Standing Committee;

(d)   requests the Standing Committee:

    i.   to prepare guidelines for the Companion Diocese Scheme after consulting with those member churches who already have guidelines;

    ii.   to undertake research to provide a set of criteria or a set of questions to assist the churches of the communion to adopt appropriate development programmes;

    iii.   to investigate the feasibility of setting up loan funds in various parts of the world to assist local churches;

(e)   acknowledges the formation of the Mission Agencies Working Group, encourages it to pursue its aims of increased Agency co-operation, and requests it to report regularly to MISAG-2. Finance will be the responsibility of the Agencies.

Statement from the Mission Agencies Conference

(a)   We affirm belief in the principle of PIM, but see the need for the process to be reviewed. There should be the possibility of greater flexibility to meet the needs of different Churches, bearing in mind that the underlying theological principle is the openness of a church to hear the Spirit's guidance in mission through a partnership with Christians of other churches. The 'First World' countries need to explore ways in which they may apply this principle more effectively.

(b)   PIM should be seen as a continuing process, with Consultations at appropriate points, rather than as a single event.

(c)   Transparency and honesty must be present throughout the whole process.

(d)   Steps should be taken to involve the whole Church in the whole PIM process, and to adopt PIM principles at all levels – parish, diocese and Province. In some cases, however, the national Church may not be the most appropriate level for holding a Consultation.

(e)   God still has much to give to his Church and we have much to receive from one another: North-North, South-South, North-South, South-North. Links should be encouraged which facilitate the sharing of vision, hope, personnel and resources.

(f)   The process of PIM may be carried out through a mission audit – the examination of the life and mission of the Church at the local or diocesan or national level.

(g)   In the planning of Consultations the following should be involved:

    i.   some external partners
    ii.   consultants with special skills.

(h)   A Consultation is not a market place – plans and projects should flow through it.

(i)   A Church should reveal all its work and, in setting priorities, review its on-going work.

(j)   Development agencies should be represented at Consultations, where appropriate, in order to focus on all aspects of mission.

(k)   In commending a greatly increased ecumenical participation, we would particularly encourage the inclusion of representatives from the widest possible spectrum of other Churches in any place.

(l)   We note the valuable role played by many inter-church and non-denominational agencies, which often have considerable Anglican involvement, but are not often part of the PIM process.

(m)   The time usually given to a Consultation needs to be extended.

(n)   PIM is an ongoing process. The follow-up to a Consultation should include:

i.   A single integrated report, not one each from the partners and the host.

ii.   A procedure for both sides of the partnership for the assessment and evaluation of action resulting from the Consultation.

iii.   The communication of the results and the assessment of the Church and its partners.

(o)   Mission Agencies should be encouraged to continue to explore ways in which representatives of Partner Churches can take part in their decision-making processes.

Comments from the Council

The Council would make the following comments to the Standing Committee regarding the statement on Partners in Mission from the Mission Agencies Conference:

(References are to *Progress in Partnership*)

(h)   Would better read: A consultation is a time for the setting of priorities not for discussing a 'shopping list'.

(j)   Realising the autonomy of the local church in choosing its external partners in any PIM consultation concern was expressed in allowing either development or mission agency representatives to be involved at the time of the setting of priorities. It was felt such agencies would be approached when the local church was seeking to realise its priorities.

(n)   The reporting procedures are unclear and in some cases unnecessary. Some mention should be made of the role of the ACC office.

Resolution 2: Terms of Reference for a New Mission Issues and Strategy Advisory Group (MISAG-2)

THAT this Council recommends the following terms of reference for MISAG-2:

(a)   to review mission issues with special reference to the theology of the mission of the Church in a pluralist society:

(b)   to explore and develop strategies of evangelism and development to help the member Churches of the Communion in their task of mission;

(c)   to review the ecumenical dimension of mission and to find ways and means for collaboration with other Christian bodies in mission;

(d)   to continue to review the Partners in Mission process;

(e)   to respond to the requests of member Churches of the Communion through the Standing Committee and to the Standing Committee's own requests for assistance in identification of needs and opportunities in evangelism and development;

(f)   to review the effectiveness of the Mission Audit as recommended by ACC-6 and to report to ACC-8;

(g)   to submit progress reports to the Standing Committee and to report to ACC-8.

3.   RENEWAL OF THE CHURCH IN MISSION – SOME ASPECTS

(a) *Renewal*

Renewal is God's gift to the Church through the Holy Spirit. Christians individually and corporately receive it by being open to the Holy Spirit and at the same time being sensitive to realities of the context in which they live. Renewal should not be confused with pietism or mere increase in the number of members of the Church. Renewal can be disturbing and it calls for a change. It comes when the Gospel is proclaimed and received, and it deepens and intensifies Christian Fellowship.

To what extent are God's people willing to put themselves at his disposal for change? In renewal there is a continuation of the divine initiative and a human response. Among both clergy and laity there may be a lack of motivation, and of concern to share the faith and to fulfil the task of evangelism. Congregations need to be willing to accept both new ideas and concepts and attitudes, and to welcome new people. Newcomers need to be made to feel that they belong and can share in the life and in the responsibilities of the Church to which they belong.

(b) *Giving Mission its Proper Place*

The MISAG Report *Giving Mission its Proper Place* to ACC-6 noted that.

> though there are notable exceptions, the dominant model of the Church within the Anglican Communion is a pastoral one. Emphasis on all aspects of the Church's life tends to be placed on care and nurture rather than proclamation and service.

Despite this assessment of the Anglican Communion by MISAG-1 we believe that its member Churches are being renewed by the Holy Spirit and are responding to their missionary vocation in various ways.

We receive the book *Open to the Spirit* as a document to be commended to the Church. These writings by a wide range of contributors tell the exciting stories of how the Holy Spirit has been constantly renewing the Church in different parts of the Communion, inspiring in it a deeper understanding of, and commitment to, God's mission in the varied contemporary contexts, and empowering members of the Church for mission.

Two of the words contrasted in the MISAG-1 Report – 'pastoral and proclamation' – present some difficulties of interpretation. 'Pastoral' conveys a rural image, the care of existing members, maintenance, one-to-one work. It involves the care of all people, not just church members, and it must therefore be the work of the whole Church, not just of the clergy. 'Proclamation' also presents similar problems of definition; 'we proclaim his promise'; but the word is not so wide as to embrace the whole of Mission. It covers the witness of the lives of individuals, not just preaching and teaching, though these certainly have a central and vital place within proclamation. 'Setting forth the work of Christ for the world' might be an adequate extension of the single word.

(c) From the experience of the churches we find that:

In *Singapore* a congregation has grown over a few years from just 35 to near 2000. This through the proclamation of the 'word' in preaching and teaching and by an inspired congregation 'gossiping the Gospel'.

In some parts of *Africa* people are demanding that the preaching is scriptural and full of teaching. Members of congregations are prepared to interrupt a preacher if they feel it necessary. One visiting English bishop preached a fifteen minute sermon. The congregation was so disappointed that they demanded their own bishop return and preach a proper sermon.

In the *United States* a parish church in the mid-west decided to heighten its image and use a series of television spots. Within a few weeks there were ninety new faces to be welcomed and brought into the life of the congregation.

In the *Sudan* where the Church is growing rapidly in a difficult political situation there is a strong accent on preaching.

By contrast in *Australia* visiting preachers are often asked to preach no longer than ten or fifteen minutes. In *England* the early service is by tradition without a sermon for the sake of those who don't want to hear one.

(d)   The churches of the Anglican Communion are churches of Word and Sacrament; between these two aspects a balance has to be fully maintained; and where out of balance, properly restored.

It is of course true that, within our sacramental services – Communion, Baptism, Confirmation – the Word is always present; provision is always made for readings, the Old Testament, the Psalms, the Epistles, the Gospels; so also in services other than the Holy Communion.

So the Word of God is proclaimed; the Communion is itself a proclamation – whenever we eat the bread and drink the cup we proclaim the Lord's death until he comes again.

(e)   *The Priority (Primacy) of Preaching*

But, within proclamation, the exposition of the Word in teaching and preaching has a central and indispensable role in renewal. This was true of our Lord's ministry –

> Jesus went about in all Galilee, teaching in their synagogues, and preaching the gospel of the kingdom, and healing ... (Matt. 4.23; 9.35).

So it stands in the great commission

> Go ye therefore and make disciples of all the nations, baptizing them ... teaching them to observe all things whatsoever I commanded you. (Matt.28.19,20).

So, too, the early Christian disciples, led by the Apostles after the Ascension

> continued stedfastly in the apostles' teaching and fellowship and in breaking of bread, and in prayers. (Acts 2.42)

The order is significant. Teaching the faith – the proclamation of the gospel – leads to fellowship; fellowship is strengthened in the breaking of bread; and breaking leads on to and is integrated with prayer in all its aspects. So also Paul to Timothy

> Till I come, give heed to reading, to exhortation, to teaching. Neglect not the gift that is in thee, which was given thee by prophecy, with the laying on of hands of the presbytery. ....Take heed to thyself, and to thy teaching. Continue in these things: for in doing this thou shalt save both thyself and them that hear thee. (1 Tim. 4.14, 16)

So also St Paul poses the eternal question:

> How then shall they call upon him in whom they have not believed?
>
> and how shall they believe in him whom they have not heard?
>
> and how shall they preach except they be sent? (Romans 10.14, 15)

From all this it is clear that in New Testament times both Jesus and the Apostles saw and practised the teaching/preaching aspect of proclamation as a very high priority.

The basic core of this proclamation is Christ and his Kingdom. To proclaim one without the other is inadequate – this is not an 'either/or'; it is a 'both/and'. We do not proclaim 'the Church' except in the context of Christ and his Kingdom

> For we preach not ourselves, but Christ Jesus as Lord, and ourselves as your servants for Jesus' sake. (2 Cor. 4.5)

(f) *The Inspiration of the Spirit in Preaching*

St Luke's narrative in the early chapters of Acts shows how the apostles first waited for the gifts of the Spirit (Acts 1.8); next they were empowered by the Spirit; and then, 'open to the spirit', they proclaimed Christ, crucified, risen and ascended. In the power of the Spirit they lived out, and proved from the first, Jesus's own words

> 'If any man thirst, let him come unto me and drink. He that believeth on me as the scripture has said, out of his belly shall flow rivers of living water.' But this spake he of the Spirit, which they that believed on him were to receive; for the Spirit was not yet given, because Jesus was not yet glorified. (John 7.37-39).

Where adequate spiritual and intellectual preparation of God's message is done, words can be taken by God and be used powerfully in the lives of the hearers. Both preachers and hearers in the delivery and reception of Proclamation need to be open to the direction of the Holy Spirit. A casual attitude is unworthy. When there is no fire in the belly of those who have accepted the responsibility of preaching, teaching and proclaiming the harvest is very thin.

(g) *Bible Emphasis*

The central authority of the Bible in our faith needs to be renewed in practice. Preaching and teaching must be more directly related to the Bible in every act of worship. There should be more systematic exposition of the Word. 'From a babe thou hast known the sacred writings which are able to make thee wise unto salvation through faith which is in Christ Jesus. Every scripture inspired by God is also profitable for teaching, for reproof, for correction, for instruction which is in righteousness that the man of God may be complete, furnished completely unto every good work'. (2 Tim. 3.15-17).

(h) *Clarity of the Message*

The message should be clear and direct. The language must be suited to the audience. There is a broad range of people who do not hear the word; it extends from those who are not told, through those who have heard in the past but have now lapsed, to those in the present congregation, whether new or more established members. The Word must be so communicated that the hearer not only hear, but receive, understand, and come to live by the message.

(i) *The Inspiration of the Spirit in Prayer*

Just as proclamation, whether preaching or teaching, needs to be Christ-centred and inspired by the Spirit, so all prayer in public and in private, should be Christ-centred and inspired by the Spirit. This is not an imposed discipline – though personal discipline is needed – but the natural reaction and activity of those who have been touched; where the Spirit of the Lord is, there is freedom (2 Cor. 3.17); and in that freedom each person's soul converses with God. This needs to be as true in public worship as in private devotion. The same openness to the Spirit is needed in prayer as in preaching. God has spoken through his Word; we need to stand on the promises of the Word in prayer, in praise, in meditation, and in preaching; and in our worship we need to allow time for listening, for waiting, for God to answer – how often in our worship do we fail to allow time for God to get a word in! In our prayers as in our preaching we share in God, and each other, the message of hope. This prayer of hope needs to be well grounded in the context of the situation. The 'Kairos Theologians' of South Africa feel that prayer has become remote from the present with all its crises. Even the contemplative needs to live in the present.

(j) *Life in Worship*

Anglicans share a tradition of prayer within set forms, though the models have become diverse and diffuse in the present generation. Nobody doubts that, at their formulation in the sixteenth/seventeenth century, the writing of the texts was permeated by the Spirit which indwelt the authors and compilers; and the Spirit can still speak through formal prayers, ancient or modern. But how often, in our public worship, do we allow the Spirit to shine through these hallowed and familar words? They have not lost their meaning and significance; but in our presentation we can, and do, often obscure them. Every reading, every prayer, including even the most familar material, needs to be most carefully prepared and presented with sensitivity and sincerity. Perfunctory, slap-dash, and ill-prepared worship is, similarly, unworthy of God and of those who come to worship Him. The Liturgy is representative – it represents the people before God and God before the people and this dramatic presentation is integral to the life of the congregation. It cannot be *replaced* by free-flowing non-liturgical forms. The Liturgy is action presenting eternity now, allowing God's people to identify themselves as Christians in the timelessness of God but set in the crisis of humankind.

(k) *The Manifestation of the Spirit within the Life of the Churches*

To say, as we do, that our preaching and teaching and prayer should all be open to the Spirit is not to embrace without question the 'charismatic' emphasis in church life; nor is it to deny it. Some see 'charismatic experience' as an expression of what ordinary language cannot convey. Some have had that experience; some may experience it; some feel they cannot share in it. The publication *Open to the Spirit* reveals the diversity of opinion on this and a tension. Within this tension there needs to be a mutual trust and respect, without imposition or denial. While personal experience needs to be tested by scripture and tradition, its value should not be underestimated;

> ...one thing I know, that whereas I was blind, now I see (John 9.25)

is a vivid witness to the certainty and simplicity of an experience which is not open to argument. If we are

> being ready always to give answer to every man that asketh you a reason concerning the hope that is in you (1 Pet. 3.15)

then those who can testify to an experience of renewal are not to be gainsaid.

(l) *The Role of the Bishops*

We return to the issue of the primacy of proclamation, and the preaching and teaching role of the clergy, especially the bishops. In their 1986 Report *The Nature of Christian Belief,* (which was sparked off by the Bishop of Durham controversy), the House of Bishops of the Church of England wrote a concluding chapter on their responsibility for the faith of the Church. They identified a two-fold task – to guard, expound and teach the faith as they have received it and to be 'apostolic pioneers' in the pursuit of which they concluded, in their final paragraph

> To give this word the attention it requires may well call for a revision of the *Church's expectation of a bishop's priorities.* If bishops are to give more leadership and guidance in the sphere of teaching and belief they will need to redesign the patterns of their work together in order to give more time to this task, and to drawing on the resources of their various theological advisory bodies. We believe this would benefit the whole Church of England; but the effects would be widely

felt, in that some things which bishops normally do at present would have to be done by others and such a change could not, therefore, be carried out without the support and co-operation of the whole church community.

Paul's injunction to Timothy, already quoted in (e) above, powerfully supports the need for the bishops to have a more open and active role as preachers and teachers of the whole gospel.

We fully endorse, for all the Churches of the Anglican Communion, that leadership and guidance in the sphere of teaching and belief as truly a part of the Apostolic Succession. It is narrowing and constricting if episcopal preaching is heavily weighted towards confirmations and inductions. There must be a risk that, where this is true, the bishops also may lose their spiritual fire in the belly. The episcopal commission is to fulfil the whole range of apostolic action, and the whole range of biblical preaching and teaching, just as much as presiding at particular 'episcopal' services. The bishops therefore need to be both 'pastors of the pastors' and 'teachers of the teachers/preachers', clerical and lay.

We encourage the bishops of the Church, as they wrestle with the demands of their office and the expectations of the clergy and people, to see how they might redesign their work patterns so they may lead in teaching and have time and space for reading, study, meditation and preparation.

(m) *The Role of the Clergy*

Any re-shaping by the bishops of the range of their activities, in order to be better able to fulfil their role as teachers, will need to be accompanied by a comparable review by the clergy of their activities. Their training, whether for two or three or five years, is to equip them theologically and practically for a preaching/teaching ministry, just as much as for pastoral work. Some, or indeed many, of the functions traditionally assumed by the clergy will need to be devolved to other hands as they too wrestle with the demands and with the expectations of the laity.

(n) *The Role of the Laity*

The demand upon bishops to redesign the patterns of their work in order to give themselves more fully to the twin tasks of teaching and preaching presupposes that such an action will develop into a process which will carry through into the entire life of the Provinces of the Anglican Communion. When that happens the life of the Church will be so changed it will no longer be a matter of one part of the Church supporting another, rather it will be one where all of God's faithful people will each discover anew their vocation and ministry that they may serve him in holiness and truth to the glory of his name.

As bishops and clergy shed those roles which are neither essentially episcopal nor priestly the laity should be found ready equipped, willing and available to accept them. This will add to our effectiveness in mission.

It is gratifying to note that there is a certain measure of lay involvement already in the liturgical life of the Provinces around the Anglican Communion. It is certainly true of most of Africa, where by sheer force of circumstances it is not possible to provide a priest for single church parishes. In this situation the role of the laymen and laywomen is quite vital.

In the field of general and financial administration more and more lay people are being involved. It is hoped that this will become increasingly so in the future as the Church's involvement in development gathers greater momentum.

The Church possesses all the resources needed for its work of mission; but an effective deployment of those resources requires a fundamental change of attitudes. This applies to the whole people of God – bishops, priests, deacons and lay people alike. In delineating the roles of ministry care needs to be taken to make sure that shared aspects of the ministry of the people of God are not forgotten.

(o)   *Signs of Decline and Growth in the Church*

The question was asked in the section why decline has set in in some provinces and there is rapid growth in others, and whether any insights can be gained by investigating the matter that should help both situations.

A small group met and wrote a short report but it was found that the subject was far too complex to be adequately dealt with by the group.

It is hoped that others might care to look at the subject in a more leisurely way and in greater depth and send any report to the Secretary General for distribution.

Resolution 3:   Renewal of the Church in Mission

THAT this Council:

(a)   expresses its gratitude to the contributors to the book of essays *Open to the Spirit*, acknowledging the value of their help in the preparation of the Provinces for the Lambeth theme, 'Renewal of the Church in Mission' and recommends it to the Lambeth Conference Mission and Ministry Preparatory Group for its consideration and commends the book to the Provinces for study.

(b)   requests the Secretary General to refer the statement above 'Renewal of the Church in Mission – Some aspects' to the Lambeth Conference Mission and Ministry Preparatory Group for its consideration.

B. MINISTRY

1. ORDINATION OF WOMEN TO THE PRIESTHOOD AND EPISCOPATE

(a) *Preamble*

i. For reasons of urgency we chose to consider the ordination of women to the priesthood and their possible consecration to the episcopate from a long list of issues concerning the Church's ministry. The reasons of urgency include the harmony and unity of the Anglican Communion, especially if or when there is a woman bishop, debates currently proceeding in churches or provinces that do not admit women to the priesthood, and our ecumenical dicussions, whether they are with churches maintaining Catholic order or with churches stemming from the Reformation.

ii. We take the most immediate concern to be the holding together, while recognising the autonomy of each, of the members of the Anglican family, particularly as we move towards the 1988 Lambeth Conference. Whether we see a woman bishop before or after the Conference, the possibility creates greater pressures on our relationships within the Anglican family than were experienced in 1978. A bishop is a focus of unity in the Catholic order of the Church, is a member of the collegial episcopal fellowship and validly confers the ordained ministry. We would not wish to underestimate the problems caused for our ecumenical relationships with those other churches that have preserved the historic Catholic order. Indeed, that concern is for many Anglicans still opposed to, or uncertain about, or even generally in favour of the ordination of women, of primary importance. Yet, as already indicated, we feel the most immediate pressure to be on unity within the Anglican Communion.

iii. From its beginning the ACC has addressed itself to the matter of women's ordination, and it may seem that it has nothing new to offer. However, we do not find in the reports of previous meetings any identification or discussion of the chief theological issues. Churches and provinces that already admit women to the priesthood may feel they have largely passed through the theological debate. For those still in the throes of synodical debate – a process that takes considerable time – it may be helpful briefly to identify the main issues. And, anyway, the ground does shift somewhat as time goes on. Our chief task, however, is to offer some help on the preservation of unity within our Communion.

(b) *Headship*

i. Emphases among the theological issues on women's ordination differ according to ecclesiastical traditions within Anglicanism. For some the primary concern comes under the principle of headship and what the Scriptures actually say about it.

ii. Two documents included in the Council's preparatory documents attempt to deal with this issue. They are *The Report of the Sydney Diocesan Doctrine Commission on the Ordination of Women to the Priesthood* and *Biblical Headship and the Ordination of Women* by Colin Craston. They attempt to deal with the same biblical evidence, and though the former document recognises that the Commission's members 'are far from having reached final and unassailable conclusions on many issues', these studies come to largely different positions. Both attempt to deal honestly with Scripture, using contemporary scholarship. They clearly reflect the Church's problem in the use and interpretation of Scripture and illustrate that it is one thing to acknowledge its authority and another thing to arrive at an agreed understanding.

iii. The authors of each document would agree that Scripture ought not to be used to provide proof-texts to undergird positions already held, and would recognise that biblical passages do not necessarily provide instant solutions to human problems and divisive issues, particularly in ages and cultures that differ greatly from those in which the Scriptures first appeared.

iv. One understanding of headship starts from the conviction that within the man-woman relationship the headship of the male is part of the order of Creation, which no development of culture or of the new Creation in Christ can change. Passages in the Pauline letters and the early chapters of Genesis are interpreted accordingly. In particular, the headship principle is applied to the teaching office in the Church, which is taken as part of the body of apostolic tradition (paradosis), which St Paul received and transmitted to the churches as having the authority of the Lord. That body of tradition, including the Gospel itself, certain standards of conduct, and certain features of church order, it is maintained, we are not at liberty to change.

v. The contrary view finds a different interpretation of the relevant Scriptures, placing emphasis on the cultural contexts, both that in which they were first given and that in which they have now to be understood. There is also a general disposition to regard any subordination of women to the headship of man as more a consequence of sin than a divinely-given principle in Creation, and to stress the changed relationships effected by Christ's redemption within the new order of his Kingdom. Baptism into Christ gives equality of standing before God (Gal. 3.28). There is said by St Paul to be 'no difference' between men and women. That cannot mean the elimination of differences in the characteristics of the sexes, but it does at least point to new developments in their partnership in Christ.

vi.   Supporters of this interpretation of the Bible also believe that where, and to whom, the Holy Scripture has given recognisable gifts for leadership the Church must not deny them but use them, regardless of the issue of gender. Unless it can be proved conclusively that a woman is barred by apostolic tradition from admission to the ministry of Word and Sacrament and pastoral leadership, the question of her admission should be determined on the basis of calling and gifts.

vii.   Understanding the Bible on the matter of headship involves complex and technical study. Prima facie meanings of isolated verses can be misleading. There is no substitute for painstaking attention to the various understandings offered, and certainly no short summary can be attempted in a report of this nature.

(c)   *'Representation' of Christ in the Church*

i.   Another theological issue is that of representation. Who can represent Christ within the fellowship of his Body? Opponents of the admission of women to the priesthood and the episcopate, both within the Anglican Communion and outside it, as the Roman Catholic Declaration, *Inter Insigniores,* and its Official Commentary, and the *Correspondence between Canterbury and Rome* (1975-6 and 1984-6) indicate, build up their arguments on the historical particularity of the Incarnation.

ii.   The fundamental question advanced here is, Why did God choose that time to be incarnate? We cannot believe it was accidental, and not a matter of deliberate choice, without questioning the sovereignty of God and the whole thrust of Scripture which speaks of the fulness of times after a period of deliberate preparation. If incarnation as a male person was determined and conditioned by the culture of the time, does this not have determinative consequences for all time in the matter of representation? Is not God saying that maleness is fundamental to that representation? Thus faith – acceptance of a fact of revealed truth – and order – the structuring of a representative ministry – are seen to be inextricably related. Jesus affirmed this understanding, it is further maintained, by choosing an all-male Apostolate, even though in other matters he was prepared to initiate change, not least in his relationship with women. And so, inasmuch as the ordained priest is seen as an ikon of Christ, particularly in the Eucharist, maleness is deemed essential to the sign.

iii.   Those who are so persuaded find additional support in their reading of the creation story in Genesis 2. Woman is there described as created after man as his helper, and comes under his leadership by virtue of him naming her. St. Paul is appealed to in 1 Corinthians 11.7 where he speaks of man reflecting the image and glory of God and woman reflecting the glory of man.

iv.   Undoubtedly it is again a difference of interpretation of Scripture and of its application to the issue of women in the ordained ministry that divides opponents and supporters. The latter put great emphasis on the destruction of walls of separation by the death and resurrection of Christ. In the new Creation inaugurated by him, human divisions, though not personal qualities and characteristics, are transcended, as has been stated previously. Furthermore, it is stressed, after his work on earth was finished, Christ ascended with the totality of our humanity to the Father. Though male in his incarnation, he bears both male and female humanity in his person at the throne of God. And even in his incarnate state, some would wish to stress, the female side of humanity was involved when, as the Christmas Preface in the 1662 Communion Service states, 'he was made man of the very substance of the Virgin Mary'.

v.   Hence, it is argued, by virtue of his assumption of our total humanity into heaven both male and female members of redeemed humanity may represent him on earth. This may apply to the specific role of presidency at the Eucharist, though many would wish to stress that it is the whole eucharistic company which represents Christ at the Eucharist rather than the one presiding. Emphasis is laid on the biblical evidence (Eph. 2.11-22; Col. 1.16-20, as well as Gal. 3.28) setting forth God's purpose of uniting all things in fellowship through Christ. Within that purpose the unity of men and women in ministry is regarded as an important factor and sign.

vi.   Even prior to his Ascension, however, Christ is described by John's Gospel as the Word becoming 'flesh' (*sarx*), the weak human condition, rather than male (*aner*), in contrast to female. Those who take these views read the Creation narratives differently from those opposed to women's ordination. They stress the complementary partnership of man and woman expressed in Genesis 1.27. Together they constitute the image of God. Within the ordained ministry, therefore, that image needs to be fully seen, the argument goes, or else it is impoverished. They also do not regard the 'help-meet' role of woman in Genesis 2 as indicating subordination, as the same word is used elsewhere of God. There is also a contrast, it is said, between naming of animals, giving them a technical description and thus establishing authority or dominion, and describing the woman as a complementary companion.

45

vii.   The choice of an all-male Apostolate is not regarded by those of this view as having permanent consequences, any more than its Jewish nationality. In the Gospel narratives, that is, prior to Pentecost, there appears to be no intention to establish Church order to any marked degree. And even if cultural considerations made the choice of males only inevitable, a new role for women, that is, in contrast with their subordinate place in Judaism, seems to be emerging. In John 11.27 Martha confesses Jesus to be the Messiah, as Peter had at Caesarea Philippi. Mary Magdalene is the first person to announce the good news of the resurrection, a central function of the Apostolate.

(d) *Development in Faith and Order*

   i.   We recognise that among those who agree that Scripture has a unique and determinative role in seeking God's will in each generation there are quite different interpretations of Scripture based on different methods. Thus we are faced today with opposing positions on the understanding of headship both in the created order and the Church, on representation of God, and in particular of the Ascended Christ, and on the significance of Jesus's choice of an all-male band of disciples.

   ii.   It therefore appears essential that we consider whether development in faith and order is a significant factor in resolving the issue of women's ordination. The promised presence and guidance of the Holy Spirit in the Church until the end of the age provide the basis for believing that the emergence of Trinitarian doctrine and the three-fold order of ministry, to mention but two matters, was in accordance with God's will. Is it possible that on the same basis we may now discern his will concerning the admission of women to the three orders?

   iii.   We must avoid the conclusion that all developments and changes in church history are divinely inspired. The church ever remains a company of sinful and fallible men and women. We ask, therefore, what criteria may be considered in determining that which is of God and that which is of the world and its standards and passions.

   iv.   CRITERIA

First and foremost we test any development by Scripture. Is it consonant with, or at least not contrary to, a balanced interpretation of the relevant biblical evidence? As Christian people honestly reading the Scriptures and acknowledging their unique and normative authority come to different answers to that question, we must move to further criteria. And here the basic question must be, what does the Holy Spirit seem to be doing in the unfolding history of humankind? The Spirit is not domesticated within the church. God's purposes are worked out in history in and through the complex affairs of sinful humanity. As from the beginning, the Spirit is still active in all the created order. Thus the church must be alert to discern developments in human society in which the Spirit is moving. Because it is in and through humankind that the developments happen, what the Spirit initiates and develops may be affected by distortions and abuse. Nevertheless a general beneficial direction may be discerned if it is of God.

v. By this understanding we may expect new things to happen in the church, new not in the sense of being a total break with the past but a development from it. Would the admission of women to the priesthood and to the episcopate be such a decisive break with the past? Opponents of the move, who would regard it in that light, base their case on their interpretation of the biblical evidence. Appealing to tradition alone, even now after nearly 2000 years, may not seem to settle the issue, for development is both possible and actual in tradition. Those who resist the development, however, have every right to challenge its advocates for positive reasons justifying it after so long a period.

vi. What opponents need to bring into consideration is the far-reaching development in the status and expanding role of women in society in modern times as a result of educational, scientific and technological advances. While for the vast majority the divinely-given role of motherhood and nurture of the family continues, opportunities for sharing with men in every realm of human life have greatly increased and will continue to do so. Extremist exploitation of this new phenomenon has been and still is evident, but examples of such should not blind us to the recognition that there is a true liberation and fuller realisation of human potential happening in our time. Christians must ask themselves; Is this of God? If it is, it must be taken as the context in which we determine the issue of women's ordination.

vii. THE UNITY OF ALL TRUTH

The underlying assumption is that truth is fundamentally one. All truth is God's truth, whether it be that which he has revealed in Scripture, and supremely in Jesus Christ to whom the Scripture bears witness, or that which humanity may discover in creation and history. And in history, as human knowledge grows in response to the promptings of the Spirit in the natural order, new situations emerge in which revealed truth in Scripture can be seen in a new light.

So, the questions to be faced include the following:

– Can the interpretation of such Scriptures as appear to be relevant to the women's ordination issue be informed by what God is now doing in human history?

47

– Are there in fact truths in Scripture which in the present context may be seen as establishing principles from which a new development in the ordained ministry is justified, a development which would not have been possible prior to the emergence of that context?

viii.   THE KINGDOM AND THE COMMUNITY OF MEN AND WOMEN

Within the development of society as we now know it, and in the light of enhanced opportunity for women's participation, does not the Gospel demand that women fully take their part in the ordained ministry as a credible sign of what the community of women and men ought to be? If the Church is the sign, earnest and instrument of the Kingdom the partnership of women and men within it should surely be a witness to the world. This is in no way to suggest that women should ape men, or to contend simply for equal opportunities, but is a recognisation that they should bring their distinctive feminine contribution to the ordained ministry of the church, and in doing so demonstrate a fuller, richer partnership.

ix.   It may be argued that, in the created order as God willed it, humankind was given a fundamental priesthood before God and on behalf of the rest of creation. Man in the generic sense was to offer to God the worship and praise of all created things and act on his behalf towards them. In that priesthood man and woman were given a complementary partnership (Genesis 1.27). From among those representing different races and cultures in this Section evidence was offered of basic philosophies of human life going back over the centuries in which the complementarity of male and female was of fundamental significance. The essential nature of a human being in cultures as far apart as Africa and East Asia was seen in being a person rather than male or female. These ancient insights may now be compared with the opening up of new frontiers of human understanding in modern times. We now realise from genetic discoveries that women and men are not so distinctively different as was once assumed. The genetic make-up of both has common and shared elements as well as distinctive. As we study the story of Creation and reflect on ancient and modern knowledge we may see evidence of the Word, the Truth, enlightening humankind in a general as well as a special revelation.

x.   Sin, however, distorted the relationship between man and woman and God, between each other, and between them and the created order. God's redeeming purpose has been to restore each of those relationships. In Christ and his work the potentiality for that purpose is given. However widely sin still abounds, grace much more abounds. And so now in God's purpose there is opportunity for a liberating development in the relationship of men and women, so that in partnership they may by God's help, if they will seek it, better fulfil their priestly responsibility in the created order. A partnership in the more specialised priesthood of the ordained ministry within the total priesthood of the whole church could, and should be, a sign to the community of all people.

(e) *Maintaining the Unity of our Communion*

i. A REVIEW

In reviewing the Lambeth Conferences of both 1968 and 1978 on the matter of the ordination of women, there was both the emphasis on continued dialogue and conversation between the Provinces of the Communion, and the calling upon the Anglican Consultative Council to initiate and implement this consultative process.

An analysis of the reports of the first six meetings of the ACC shows the response made to this basic request of 'initiating and implementing a consultative process'. Only in ACC-I Limuru, did the Council give direct advice to any one Church within the Communion when it responded to the Bishop of Hong Kong regarding his desire to ordain a woman: 'this Council advises the Bishop of Hong Kong, acting with the approval of his Synod, and any other bishop of the Anglican Communion acting with the approval of his Province, that, if he decides to ordain women to the priesthood, his action will be acceptable to this Council; and that this Council will use its good offices to encourage all Provinces of the Anglican Communion to continue in communion with these dioceses'.

Reviewing ACC-2 Dublin, it appears that the action of ACC-1 was questioned, as the authority and role of the Anglican Consultative Council was brought into clearer focus: 'As its name states, the Council is a *Consultative* body. It does not legislate. It can inform members of each other's actions and can advise any Church on specific matters of concern'.

Following this direction the Council in its subsequent meetings has seen its role as being principally in helping the Churches in a consultative process that shares the experiences of the Communion; and reflecting on the overall process as it relates to the question of the autonomy of each Province in the unity that we share and seek both within the Anglican Communion and with other Churches.

This meeting of ACC-7 has seen its continued role in the consideration of the ordination of women as primarily addressing itself to one major question.

As already indicated we believe that the major question for the Anglican Communion today is how we maintain our unity as each Province continues to discern the will of God for its life in mission in the consideration of the ordination of women. As the process continues both within the individual Provinces and collectively in the Communion, how are the opinions/convictions of both sides accommodated? When a Province decides to ordain women how are those who disagree held within the family of that Province? If a Province decides against the ordination of women or if it is still in the process of making that decision, how might that Province recognize the total ministry of one that has proceeded with the ordination of women?

We believe the Anglican Communion in its struggle with this issue is in a period of its life that is willing to live with its disagreements, but we raise the question as to how long this period will last before the disagreements are accepted as part of the diversity within the Communion. The reality of our diversity must be faced and the respect for the integrity of both positions recognized.

ii.   SOME EXPERIENCES FROM THE CHURCH

We acknowledge the experiences and benefits within those Churches and Provinces that do ordain women. We note that a substantial majority within them, despite initial anxieties and divisions, gratefully testify to the beneficial effects of women in the priesthood. And we note that the original fears of division have not been realized. We share the following information, drawn from leaders in the Provinces concerned and expressed in their own words.

a)   Brazil

The legislation authorising the ordination of women to all three orders of ministry took ten years to complete. It was then approved almost unanimously (only 1 clerical and 1 lay vote against). All bishops are committed to the ordination of women.

At the present time there is some opposition at parish level to having a woman rector, but a woman priest can preach and celebrate even in such a parish.

At this time one woman is in charge of a parish where traditionally 'machismo' is strong. Another woman is in charge of a mission. Both are accepted by their male colleagues. An earlier opponent of the ordination of women in the Provincial convention now accepts women priests.

A tension in another realm is located between those who are involved in the charismatic renewal and the traditionalists and between those influenced by liberation theology. The effort to overcome this tension may be applicable in the ordination issue. It may be outlined in this way:

(1) An emphasis on fellowship rather than personal doctrinal affirmations. The Church is the people of God.

(2) Growth towards the acceptance of diversity in unity. There is some evidence that we can accept this divergence as our Anglican way. So we can diverge but keep fellowship. We adhere to this principle.

(3) With regard to other Provinces which do not ordain women we are not neutral. We sent a woman priest to the ministry of women celebration in England. We did this on the principle that we are a world-wide fellowship, which regards divergence as natural. In this way we witness to what we interpret as the Gospel.

b) Canada

Some of the steps taken in Canada are below:

(1) The decision to ordain was first accepted 'in principle' only. This gave time for reflection and discussion at diocesan level.

(2) We passed a 'conscience clause' to protect those opposed to the acceptance of a woman's priestly ministry.

(3) To ensure the integrity of the conscience clause no woman priest presides at a diocesan or provincial eucharist.

(4) We caution the women about visiting any diocese without the explicit permission of the bishop.

(5) We have tried to prepare the ordained women for the hurts they may experience and at the same time sought to make them sensitive to the hurts of the objectors.

With ten years of experience there continues to be harmony. We perceive only isolated evidence of insensitivity, minimal separation of the Church, and the widespread growth in the acceptance of women ordained to the priesthood throughout Canada.

The Canadian House of Bishops with regard to the consecration of a woman to the episcopate has agreed unanimously that the consecration can proceed, although one of them is in fact himself unwilling to ordain a woman to the priesthood.

c) New Zealand

A General Synod commission established to study the question of the ordination of women and to advise the Church recommended that legislation be prepared for the ordination of women to the priesthood.

The Province had earlier provided for the ordination of women to the diaconate. The General Synod legislation of 1976 was supported by large majorities and it received the required sanctions from diocesan synods. Two diocesan bishops were hesitant or opposed. One of these decided to accept the decision of the Church later, the other continued to be privately opposed and did not ordain any women until this year. (He did not make any public statement on his position). The passage of time during which his position was understood and accepted led to a change of mind.

There has been no organised or significant opposition to the decision and no clerical defections because of it. The close fellowship of the bishops was not affected by the issue.

At General Synod 1986 legislation was introduced to remove any doubt that women could be constitutionally consecrated to the episcopate. No opposition is expected.

d) USA

The legislation of the General Convention of 1976 authorising the ordination of women was preceded by more than ten years of study and debate. Since 1976 approximately 900 women have been ordained to the priesthood and 350 to the permanent diaconate. The experience and contribution of women in the ordained ministry over the past eleven years in the life of the Church has been so positive that the House of Bishops in 1985 voted overwhelmingly that it would not withhold consent for a person elected to the office of bishop because of gender.

The serious divisions that were supposed to develop because of the ordination of women did not materialise. Although there were bishops who opposed the decision none defected and only 0.7% of the clergy and 0.5% of the laity left the Church. It is difficult to give definitive numbers within the dissident churches but it is estimated that there are about 15,000 members which is 0.62% of the episcopalian population. There are less than three hundred clergy which is 2.1% of the total number of clergy in the Church.

The bishops meeting in 1977 voted to enact a conscience clause to protect the integrity of everyone's convictions on this issue. It has enabled the unity of our House of Bishops to continue in a sensitive respect for one another. In 1976 15-20 bishops out of a house of 150 opposed the ordination of women but today not more than twelve of its active bishops are opposed.

With the likelihood of a woman in the episcopate the House of Bishops is currently seeking ways for those opposed to this issue to stay within the Communion. This study will be reported to the House of Bishops in September 1987.

(f) *Recommendations to help maintain Unity*

Following from these examples we suggest that there are certain elements necessary for a commitment to and strategy for maintaining our unity.

The following recommendations are concerned with relations within a Province, relations between Provinces, the role of the Archbishop of Canterbury, and women in the episcopate.

i. WITHIN A PROVINCE

a) The bishops commit themselves to remain in communion with each other with the understanding that no-one be forced to ordain a woman.

b) It follows that in the life of the Church's ministry pastoral consideration be given to the end that no member of the Church, either lay or ordained, be forced to accept the priestly ministry of a woman.

c) There should be agreement between the bishops of a Province that a woman seeking to test her vocation would not be disqualified because her bishop takes an opposing view. In such a case she would be encouraged to approach another bishop.

d) The decision of a bishop to ordain or not to ordain should not come between the bishop's pastoral office and his responsibility to parishes and clergy of the diocese. The bishop exercising his pastoral responsibility should not deny a visit to any parish in his diocese which might be in opposition to his conviction and conversely no parish should deny an episcopal visit for the same reason.

ii. PROVINCE TO PROVINCE

a) The Provinces commit themselves to remain in communion with one another regardless of their decision on the ordination of women.

b) Within these early years there is a particular need for sensitivity between the Provinces, and where possible, the mutual acceptance of the priestly ministry of women. We encourage bishops who have ordained women not to force the issue in a spirit of confrontation but to respect the integrity of the decision-making processes of each Province.

c) Through the ACC regular consultation should be established between all the Provinces on this issue. This consultation would enable the Provinces to share their experiences, and to offer and receive advice and counsel from each other. This consultation process could take many forms such as Primate to Primate, between ministry commissions, and any other configuration which might be helpful. We believe this consultation process would be stimulated as we reaffirm resolution 23B of ACC-6.

iii. THE ARCHBISHOP OF CANTERBURY

The Archbishop of Canterbury as President of the Anglican Consultative Council should continue to use his good offices to bring the Provinces into the consultative process. We believe his broad experience and knowledge of the Communion in all its diversity will be a great encouragement to everyone.

iv. WOMEN IN THE EPISCOPATE

The possibility of the consecration of a woman to the episcopate needs serious consideration in the Anglican Communion. Admission of women to the order of deacon and priest in some Provinces of the Communion is already judged as eligibility for the entry of women to the historic three-fold order. It is therefore logical that women be admitted to the order of bishop. That however will have far-reaching consequences for the Anglican Communion and would raise the following questions:

a) Would other bishops within a Province and those in all the Provinces of the Communion recognize and accept a woman bishop?

b) Would ordinations and consecrations by a woman bishop be held valid in the diocese, in the Province and in the other Provinces of the Anglican Communion?

c) Would unacceptability of consecrations and ordinations performed by a woman bishop raise the question of the impairment or validity of the episcopal orders of those who consecrated the woman bishop?

d) Would consecration of a woman bishop in any Province of the Anglican Communion jeopardise the continuing negotiations with the Roman Catholic and Orthodox Churches?

e) Would it fracture the Communion should some dioceses or Provinces not accept a woman bishop?

In response to such questions it may be hoped that, just as the Communion has survived the entry of women to the three-fold order at the level of the diaconate and presbyterate, so would it survive the entry of women to the episcopate. The same may be the case with the future of the relationships with the Orthodox and Roman Catholic Churches. This will require great sensitivity on the part of all concerned. When new pressures are felt within a family, truthfulness and concern for the deep feelings of all its members are equally essential, if it is to hold together.

In the first place the Communion will have to develop the same kind of response of tolerance as it did in the case of women priests, then of understanding and, eventually, of universal acceptance for the enrichment and fulfilment of the historic three-fold order of the sacred ministry.

v. THE ORDINATION OF WOMEN AND ECUMENICAL RELATIONS

It will be clear that we have spent most of our discussion on the issue of maintaining our unity within the Communion. We are aware that we have disappointed the Roman Catholic, Orthodox and Old Catholic Churches in ordaining women but we wish to make it clear in the words of Lambeth 1978:

a)   that the holding together of diversity within a unity of faith and worship is part of the Anglican heritage;

b)   that those who have taken part in ordinations of women to the priesthood believe that these ordinations have been into the historic ministry of the Church as the Anglican Communion has received it; and

c)   that we hope the dialogue between these other Churches and the member Churches of our Communion will continue because we believe that we still have understanding of the truth of God and his rule to learn from them as together we all move towards a fuller catholicity and deeper fellowship in the Holy Spirit.

We express our gratitude at the initiative taken by the Archbishop of Canterbury by putting this subject on the agenda of ARCIC II. We are further grateful for the Archbishop's clear articulation of the Anglican position in his letter to Pope John Paul II in December 1985 and his correspondence with Cardinal Johannes Willebrands in the same month.

vi.   We welcome the setting up by the Primates at their meeting in March 1986 of the Working Group on Women in the Episcopate, chaired by the Primate of Australia, Archbishop John Grindrod, and look forward to its report.

Ordination of women deacons in Canterbury Cathedral

Resolution 4: Ordination of Women to the Priesthood and the Episcopate

THAT this Council:

(a) commends the section of the report entitled 'Ordination of Women to the Priesthood and Episcopate' to the Provinces and to the relevant Section at the Lambeth Conference;

(b) encourages all Provinces to be sensitive to one another in this matter;

(c) encourages all Provinces to be sensitive to ordained women and to women whose hopes for ordination have not been realised;

(d) expresses its appreciation and support of the Archbishop of Canterbury in his role of encouraging the consultative process between the Provinces;

(e) requests the Secretary General to obtain and circulate to the Provinces information on the state of the debate in Provinces where women have not been ordained to the priesthood and the degree of reception where they have.

2.   LITURGY AND THE LAITY

Ministration of the Holy Communion

ACC-6 discussed the problems which arise in situations where scarcity of clergy makes the maintenance of eucharistic worship difficult; they noted that various solutions have been practised or suggested:

(a)   administration by a licensed lay leader from the reserved sacrament (though they observed that some provinces would not find the practise acceptable).

(b)   licensing by the bishop of a lay leader to preside and celebrate at the Eucharist (though they noted that this practice is at present very rare).

(c)   the ordination of a local priest to meet the need.

ACC-6 was convinced that the Anglican tradition of priests presiding at the Eucharist should be upheld, and stated 'at the time' a clear preference for the ordination of local priests; they nevertheless commended the subject for further discussion at ACC-7 and Lambeth 1988 (*Bonds of Affection*, p 67, 7.7).

Neither of the terms 'Lay Presidency at the Eucharist', nor 'Lay Celebration of the Eucharist' are very adequate. All worshippers, clergy or lay, 'celebrate' and this is not a term which should be appropriated to any one person; and a lay person cannot 'preside' in the commonly understood sense of consecrating the elements. For the purpose of this discussion, we use the term 'Lay Ministration of the Communion' which is quite distinct from lay assistance at the Communion.

We endorse the previous view of ACC-6 that the Anglican tradition of priests presiding at the Eucharist should continue to be upheld at this time and that licensing by the bishop of a lay leader for the purpose of ministering the Communion in full should not be encouraged.

But we note that the practice of duly authorised laity administering 'sick' communion in homes from the Reserved Sacrament is gaining acceptance. We also note that, in the new draft of the New Zealand Prayer Book, explicit provision is made for lay Ministration from the Reserved Sacrament, with the rubric that the whole Prayer of Consecration is to be omitted. Brazil also acts in this way. We understand that the practice would embrace both sick communion and where appropriate extension to remote sub-congregations; it might also include deferred communion within the same congregation, which we understand happens in Canada. It seems to some that the use of the Reserved Sacrament in this way attempts to solve problems which might otherwise be solved in more theologically sound ways.

Some of the issues raised are as follows:

i. Can a lay person properly administer the Reserved Sacrament
   a) for a sick person or in an emergency?
   b) for extended communion in a sub-congregation?
   c) for deferred communion in the same place?

ii. What is the status of the congregation in the context of the Eucharistic Prayer?

iii. Can the Words of Institution or the whole Eucharistic Prayer be used by a lay person and in what circumstances.
   a) in full?
   b) in an amended form?
   c) not used at all or replaced by a different prayer?

iv. What is the understanding of 'intention' in the saying of the Eucharistic Prayer? Can a Eucharistic Prayer including the words of institution be said either with or without the intention of consecrating the elements?

Resolution 5: Liturgy and the Laity

THAT this Council asks the Secretary General to refer to the Liturgical Network the statement 'Liturgy and the Laity – Ministration of the Holy Communion' and asks the network to consider the issues raised in it and report to ACC-8.

3. THE DIACONATE

ACC-6 discussed developments in the diaconate and diaconal ministry (*Bonds of Affection*, pp 68/69, 7.7), and 'wished to encourage the process in which the diaconate is seen as an order of servanthood ministry ..... directly under the bishop .....' ACC-6 saw that in renewal of the diaconate careful thought would have to be given to selection, training, and its place within the polity. They observed that 'the deacon is found in some cases in the lay order and in orders within the clergy order'.

ACC-6 asked that the review of the diaconate be a priority for study at ACC-7. As there is no material at hand this cannot be done. Nonetheless it appears there is no evidence that the diaconate is found in the lay order in this church, nor is there any significant support for that concept.

Resolution 6: The Diaconate

THAT this Council asks the Secretary General to assemble material from all provinces about reviews which have been made or are in hand concerning the diaconate, particularly about steps which are being contemplated about 'a distinct order of servanthood ministry'. This to be done by the end of 1987 so it might be considered at Lambeth in 1988 and ACC-8.

Section II – Dogmatic and Pastoral Affairs

A. FOR THE SAKE OF THE KINGDOM

1. CHRIST AND CULTURE

We warmly welcome this report from the Inter-Anglican Theological and Doctrinal Commission as an illuminating and balanced discussion of some central theological issues, useful for provoking further reflection and discussion.

On the substantive issues discussed in the report we wish to make the following affirmations, doing so in a way which draws directly on the experiences of the group as they have been shared with one another. We concentrated on the relationship between Christ and culture. The report considers this within the context of the relationship between the Church as experienced and the Kingdom as anticipated.

(a) There is that in every culture to which we can say 'Yes'.

By culture we mean the language, history, stories, customs, lifestyle, accumulated wisdom and religion into which we are born, by which we are shaped and through which we find our identity as human beings. Through this culture, which is not static but ever-changing, God is making us. To say 'Yes' to culture is to say 'Yes' to God our creator.

For example, in India we would want to say 'Yes' to the traditional respect for life, for all religions and to the stress on family unity.

(b) There is that in every culture which answers to Christ and finds its fulfilment in Christ.

For example in Chinese society Confucius taught that human beings are brothers and sisters. In Christ, through seeking the will of God, this possibility becomes a reality. Again, in Chinese society the concept of TAO well translates the LOGOS of the prologue to John's Gospel and does so in such a way that the meaning is kept close to the Hebrew background. To take another example, the naturally accepted racial mix and racial tolerance of the Seychelles answers to the Christian proclamation that in Christ there is neither Jew nor Greek, male nor female, slave nor free. Or again, in African tribal religions there is the concept of a supreme God which finds its fulfilment in Hebrew monotheism.

It should also be noted that in some societies there are counter-religious movements that express the divine will.

(c)   There is that in every culture which is challenged by Christ.

The culture into which we are born and by which we are shaped does not come straight from the hands of the creator. It comes spoiled and distorted by human sin. For example in India certain cultural and social manifest-ations of the caste system and in particular the existence of outcasts are con trary to the Gospel. In many parts of the world, the Church, by working for human rights, the enhanced status of women, for adequate health care and universal education, challenges the assumptions of societies in which these are matters of indifference. Corruption is present in most countries in the world. Corrupt practices are exposed and judged by the light of Christ.

The challenge to a society may be painful, not simply because we want to cling on to what is wrong, but because some traditional mores preserve genuine values. For example, in Papua New Guinea the custom of favour-ing one's own tribe in business dealings is challenged by more universal notions of fairness brought by the Gospel. Yet, traditional methods encourage loyalty, and cement tribal solidarity.

(d)   The interaction of the Church in one cultural form with another culture should bring about a change in outlook and lifestyle for both parties to the interaction.

(This is what we take *For the Sake of the Kingdom* to mean by their use of the word 'repentance', though we would lay more stress than they do on change of lifestyle. Repentance is more than a change of mind.)

This change has two aspects.

First, the Church, which is inevitably and properly embedded in a particular culture (the incarnational principle), comes, through contact with another culture, to a wider and profounder vision of the universal Christ. The Church seeks to listen to and learn from the voice of Christ in that other culture; deep calls unto deep. Europe simply received the Gospel from Western Asia. More recently, as African and Asian cultures opened them-selves to Christ in European culture, so now European and North American Christians are opening themselves to learn from the Christ of African and Asian cultures.

Secondly, this openness brings about a realisation of the partial perspective of any one Church and a willingness to have that partial perspective corrected by the view from a different vantage point. So, the Western Church, embedded in an excessively individualistic Western culture, can rediscover the communal nature of the Church through contact with African societies. Or again, they can recognise a difference in the quality of poverty, East and West.

Countries that are economically poor may be humanly rich. Wealthy countries sometimes contain abject human misery.

This willingness to be open to other cultures, to be enriched and corrected by them, is properly called repentance, a word with moral overtones, because it is an attempt to counteract the tendency to absolutize the forms in which the Gospel comes to us. Where this repentance has not happened the consequences have been painful for humanity and the Church. Not only is there the long history of hurt done to colonized cultures by the Church in league with empire, the Church also has lost out. One example might be the failure of the Church in the sixteenth century to Christianize properly the Chinese cult of ancestors. There is space within the Church, as Matteo Ricci and others argued, not least in the doctrine of the communion of saints, to encompass such customs, at least in an altered form. But disputes between religious orders led to a rejection of any attempt at accommodation and the failure of Christianity in China at that time.

2. BELIEF AND DISBELIEF IN THE MODERN WORLD

During the 1960s it was widely alleged that we now have a secular culture in Europe and North America. However some sociologists challenged this, pointing out for example that a very high percentage of people read their horoscopes. During the 1970s and 80s, with the interest in the occult and the rise of fundamentalist forms of religion throughout the world, the idea that we now live in a secular world seems even less convincing. Recent opinion polls show Australia, an apparently secular country, to be very religious. It may be that in the decades ahead the main threat to authentic Christian faith will be bad religion rather than secularism. In countries where there is a militant Islam or a resurgent Hinduism a secular state would be much welcomed by Christians. In the West the cults and new religious movements, some of them claiming to be Christian, are growing.

There is another consideration. There is much in modern industrial and technological society to which Christians wish to respond positively; for it is the product of God-given intelligence and inquisitiveness.

There is an apparent paradox here. For as there has been a religious resurgence, so, at the same time, there has been a growing disbelief in any religion amongst some other people. Figures suggest that those who claim no religion are growing faster than any religious group. This disbelief is now a major problem amongst the young emerging élites in the developing world. Students go to university and, whether it is abroad or in their own country, they too often come back dismissive of religion. This is true even of children brought up in devout Christian homes. The causes of this are various. There is the advent of Western capitalism and materialism. The 'yuppie' (Young, Upwardly mobile, Professional People) mentality is not confined to Europe and North America. Many of the best educated in the developing world are pursuing material goals, and have little thought for spiritual matters. In some countries the Government is Marxist and in a variety of ways, subtle and unsubtle, opposes the influence of religion on the assumption that man is his own maker. Then, at universities, there is sometimes a clash between nineteenth century views of science and over-literal interpretations of Christianity. A battle that elsewhere was fought and won many decades ago is still being waged with antique weapons. Even when the relationship between religion and science is correctly understood, the sheer achievement of modern technology can seem a threat to religion.

These considerations point to the following conclusions. First that the Churches, not least in the developing world, need to pay careful attention to their ministry to students and teachers in universities and institutes of higher education. A great deal of careful educational work and pastoring of students as they think through their faith in the light of modern knowledge is needed. Secondly, the training of the clergy must constantly be borne in mind. The witness of the Christian faith depends not only on authenticity of life but on the intellectual credibility of the faith to the best educated members of society. This includes not only theoretical questions but the thoughtful attempt to relate the Christian faith to the secular concerns of politics and economic development.

STYLE

For the Sake of the Kingdom raises questions not only in relation to its content but in relation to its style. The report itself notes that it is written in an abstract style and urges the job of 'translation' on to the Churches. But in order to be translated it must first be understood. The group studying the report found difficulty in this and this would certainly be the case with most Church members including many Church leaders. We therefore recommend that in future the ACC tries to produce reports in a unified and accessible style, bearing in mind that for many members of the Anglican Communion English, French, Spanish, Portugese or Japanese may not be their first language. It has been pointed out that the use of a special vocabulary to speak of the things of God is a modern Western phenomenon. Before the seventeenth century Christian language knew no distinction between 'secular' and 'religious' terminology. To take one tiny example, the word prayer has become a technical term. But in some contexts the secular word 'ask' could say what was meant more directly and understandably. A theologian has been well defined as a person who watches his language in the presence of God. This watching is also a wrestling, akin to the struggle with words of a poet; not the attempt to prettify a style, but to think more clearly and feel more deeply about the issues in question.

Resolution 7: Inter-Anglican Theological and Doctrinal Commission

THAT this Council

(a)   welcomes warmly the Report of the Inter-Anglican Theological and Doctrinal Commission *For the Sake of the Kingdom* as an illuminating and balanced discussion of some central theological issues;

(b)   commends it for study within the Anglican Communion but acknowledges that for many, at the local level, help in the way of a study guide will be necessary. A simple study guide, drawn up by people of very diverse cultures is offered; (See Appendix to this Section)

(c)   recommends that the Standing Committee gives thought to the difficult problem of producing reports that can be understood by those for whom the language of the report is their second language;

(d)   recommends that the Churches, not least in the developing world, pay careful attention to their ministry to students and teachers in Universities and Institutes of Higher Education;

(e)   recommends to the Churches and institutes of theological education of the Communion that clergy be trained to understand the trends in society towards secularisation, affecting in various ways all cultures, and to relate the Gospel to all levels of modern society, not least to the well educated.

B. INTER-FAITH RELATIONSHIPS

1. DIALOGUE AND INTER-RELIGIOUS ENCOUNTER

ACC-6 reviewed the Board for Mission and Unity (BMU) report of the Church of England *Towards a Theology for Inter-Faith Dialogue* and qualified its welcome with the judgement that it was too 'academic'. It was republished with an additional chapter by Bishop Michael Nazir-Ali and was submitted to ACC-7 with a compilation of responses. We have appreciated the supplemented BMU report and found the compilation of responses to it, entitled *Yes and No,* helpful. Both can be warmly recommended for pre-Lambeth reading.

Real dialogue, not just at a theoretical level but in the meeting of persons, will be of vital importance in the decades ahead. In countries where Christians live with people of other religions it is essential from the point of view of social harmony that they come to understand and appreciate one another better. From an ethical point of view loving our neighbour means trying to enter into their mind and feelings and to understand the world from their point of view. The theological basis for dialogue varies and we do not wish to go over that debate again here. But it is the conviction of those who produced *For the Sake of the Kingdom* that there is that in every culture to which we can say 'Yes'; and most cultures include religious ideas and images.

However, vital though dialogue is, we would want to stress that the situation in different countries varies enormously, and that some kinds of contact with certain religious practices can be definitely harmful for Christians. Examples have been put before us of Christians becoming possessed as a result of trying to combine their Christian faith with elements drawn from the superstitious aspects of religion. We are anxious that Anglican encounter with other religions should not be considered only from a European or North American point of view but that it should take into account the experience, both positive and negative, of Christians in Africa, Asia and Latin America.

Resolution 8: Inter-Faith Relations

THAT this Council:

(a) welcomes the implementation of Resolution 20 of ACC-6 and notes that a Co-ordinator of Anglican/Muslim relations has now been appointed. We recommend that Resolution 20 be implemented in full. Areas that should continue to be examined would include ways in which the two communities can better live together, the application of Sharia, mutual respect and freedom of religion.

(b)   recommends that the Lambeth Conference, after studying this subject, get in touch with the ACC about setting up a continuing body to study Inter-Religious encounter especially in the light of African and Asian and Latin American perspectives.

2.   JEWISH-CHRISTIAN RELATIONS

There are two reasons why Jewish-Christian relations need to be handled with special care and sensitivity. Firstly, Judaism and Christianity are both hewn from the same rock, the people of God of the Hebrew scriptures; and both communities appeal to those scriptures to discern the mind and will of God: secondly, because of the tragic history of past relationships, culminating in the holocaust, a history poisoned by much anti-Jewish feeling.

Resolution 9:   Jewish-Christian Relations

THAT this Council:

recommends that the Secretary General of the ACC draw up a set of guidelines on Jewish-Christian relations, drawing on existing sets, and that these be offered to the 1988 Lambeth Conference for discussion and commendation.

C. CHRISTIAN INITIATION

ACC-6 resolved that the issues of admission of children to communion prior to Confirmation and Confirmation as commissioning for ministry and service be considered for study in the Provinces in the next three years (1984-87), and also that the Agenda for ACC-7 take them into account in preparation for Lambeth 1988.

1. ADMISSION TO HOLY COMMUNION PRIOR TO CONFIRMATION

We have received a variety of responses from the Provinces. Broadly speaking it is permitted to admit baptised children to Holy Communion after appropriate instruction in Australia, Brazil, Liberia, New Zealand, Scotland and Southern Africa; and also in Canada and the USA (though see below). In England some dioceses give permission in certain parishes.

The matter is being discussed in South America, England, Uganda, Japan, Jerusalem and the Middle East, and the West Indies but not yet in Burma.

We have no information from five Provinces.

Although Central Africa has a pilot scheme the Province has declared that it is not at the point of admitting children to Communion. There is no change in traditional practice in Ireland and the South Pacific. In Wales the issue is under discussion but parishes so far consulted seem to be opposed.

Overall it is apparent that there is increasing movement towards the admission of children to Communion prior to Confirmation but the trend is by no means universal. This is hardly surprising: practice is almost inevitably uneven, granted the wide variety of cultural conditions and different theological perceptions. Nevertheless we hope that those Provinces which are currently discussing the issue and those other Provinces which have not sent ACC any information will provide progress reports by early 1988. This will enable the Lambeth Conference to give a fuller appraisal than the ACC can provide at this stage.

The Boston Consultation. Since ACC-6 an inter-Anglican liturgical consultation has taken place in Boston, USA, in July 1985 producing a statement on Children and Communion.

Its principal recommendation is that since baptism is the sign of full incorporation, all baptised persons should be admitted to Communion. 'It is paradoxical to admit children to membership in the body of Christ through baptism, and yet to deny that membership in the eucharistic meal that

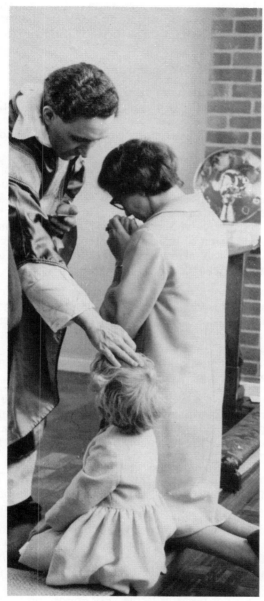

Children and Communion

69

follows'. The statement argues that admission to Communion at the age of nine, seven or five may tend to institutionalise the 'minimum age' threshold, and fails to take baptism sufficiently seriously as incorporation into eucharistic life.

'The baptised life in Christ is a eucharistic life.'

The Statement goes on to recommend that provincial baptismal rites be reviewed so that texts explicitly affirm the communion of the newly baptised, and that only one rite be authorised for baptism whether of adults or infants so that no essential distinction be made between persons on basis of age.

In the United States it has been accepted since 1970 that Baptism is the sole basis for Christians to be admitted to Holy Communion, and the American Book of Common Prayer (1979) provides for this principle. The practice is growing and becoming more widespread. The principle is implicit in the Canadian Book of Alternative Services (1985), though the common practice seems to be the admission of baptised children who have received pastoral instruction and made a simple statement of faith. In most dioceses children younger than seven are admitted.

In England the *Knaresborough Report,* currently being debated, concludes that it is permissible for the baptised to be admitted to Holy Communion. And in New Zealand, as Archbishop Brian Davis's paper circulated to ACC members demonstrated, the Boston proposals are being seriously studied. Bishop Colin Bazley of Chile also sent us a paper advocating admission to communion following baptism, but his proposals had not at that time been submitted to his Diocesan Executive Council.

The Boston proposals, with their appeal to the practice of the early Church, do mark a radical break with the tradition of the Western Church for many centuries by requiring neither instruction nor profession of faith on the part of the candidate in his or her own name before admission to Holy Communion.

There is, however, a growing view, illustrated by the BEM Report and other Anglican reports and papers (e.g. Knaresborough) that baptism is the full and complete sacrament of incorporation into Christ and the Church.

This understanding of the sacramental rite of baptism does not deny that incorporation into Christ involves a process of growth and development, irrespective of the age of the candidate. For the baptised infant there is an expectation that he/she will receive Christian nurture and make a public and responsible profession of faith at a later date. Confirmation provides an opportunity, but not necessarily the only opportunity, for such a faith response.

However, not all agree that the case for these proposals has been established, or that the rationale of the traditional Anglican practice has been adequately appreciated. There are unresolved questions:-

Does not the sequence of Baptism-Confirmation-Admission to Holy Communion rightly imply that baptism is not a complete rite of initiation when it lacks a public affirmation of faith by the candidate in his/her own name, with the prayer of the bishop representing the wider church?

Does not the limitation of the sacrament of initiation to water baptism reduce the full character of the sacrament?

Does not the Boston approach require a tightly drawn baptismal policy, while pastoral and cultural circumstances in the Provinces of the Communion vary considerably?

What effect has the new approach to initiation had on the number of candidates being confirmed, the frequency of confirmation services, and on the role of the bishop in the initiation rites?

Are not the disciplinary requirements for receiving the sacrament (as set out e.g. in the invitation 'Ye that do truly...') and the danger of unworthy receiving (as enjoined in 1 Corinthians 11) inconsistent with participation in the sacrament by infants and children who have not reached years of discretion?

We have seen (above) that the 'mind' of the Anglican Communion is not yet fully determined nineteen years after the resolution of the 1968 Lambeth Conference concerning the admission of children to communion after appropriate instruction. It is clear that a substantial amount of time must be allowed for the more far-reaching Boston proposals to receive careful theological, liturgical and pastoral examination in the Provinces of the Anglican Communion.

2. CONFIRMATION AS COMMISSIONING FOR MINISTRY AND SERVICE

There is inherent in the Anglican tradition an understanding that Confirmation is a strengthening for Christian witness and service. Our liturgies reflect this. In Provinces where baptised infants or children are being admitted to Communion, confirmation is seen not as the completion of baptism but as an acknowledgement and celebration of what baptism means and promises. And it tends to become an event in adult life, with the emphasis placed on being empowered by the Holy Spirit (through prayer and laying-on-of-hands by the bishop) for responsible witness and service, as well as being an opportunity for a mature affirmation of faith.

Resolution 10:   Christian Initiation

THAT this Council

(a)   requests the Secretary General to facilitate and encourage continuing study of the pastoral, educational, liturgical and theological implications of initiation reform; requests further that, where practicable, he should encourage those Provinces with experience of a new approach to initiation and admission to communion to share that experience with Provinces which follow the traditional pattern;

(b)   commends for study in the context of this subject the Lima text of *Baptism, Eucharist and Ministry* (World Council of Churches) and the statement of the International Anglican Consultation (Boston, July 1985) on Children and Communion;

(c)   requests the Secretary General to draw the attention of member Churches to the growing number of educational resources that are available in the Anglican Communion for the nurture and instruction of candidates for Baptism (and their sponsors), admission to Communion and Confirmation;

(d)   requests that this report be referred to the Lambeth Conference for study and comment.

D. LITURGICAL MATTERS

The preparatory papers for the Dogmatic and Pastoral section included the statement of an International Anglican Consultation held in Boston in July 1985 on Children and Communion, and a note from the Bishop of Winchester recommending that the second such Consultation planned for August in Northern Italy on Liturgical Education and Formation be 'recognised' by the ACC, and that its successors be accorded some kind of official status.

Resolution 11:   International Anglican Liturgical Consultations

THAT this Council:

(a)   recognises the 1987 Consultation, which is not to be funded by the ACC, and requests that its proceedings be made available to the ACC and the Lambeth Conference 1988;

(b)   recommends that the membership of future consultations be widely representative of the Communion, and that the Secretary General be requested to confer with the organisers about its future meetings;

(c)   encourages Provinces to give financial support for members of their Province who attend such gatherings.

E. PROPOSAL FOR AN ANGLICAN COMMUNION LITURGICAL COMMISSION

Thirty years ago in preparation for the 1958 Lambeth Conference, Archbishop Geoffrey Fisher prefaced a preparatory document *Principles of Prayer Book Revision* with the statement:

> Every Lambeth Conference from 1897 onwards has referred to the Book of Common Prayer as holding a cardinal place in the unity of the Anglican Communion, as providing a norm of its worship and a classical expression of its doctrine. (p.ix)

However, the Archbishop noted that over the years there had been increasing anxiety 'lest in the proper and laudable provision of variations to suit national and local circumstances' there might be a tendency to stray too far from the norm and that consequently the place of the Prayer Book as the common possession and standard of the whole Communion might be imperilled.

The Lambeth Conference of 1958 (Resolutions 73-76 *The Lambeth Conference 1958,* 1.47 ff.) in commending the report to the careful study of the Anglican Communion called attention to 'those features in the Book of Common Prayer which are essential to the safeguarding of our unity'. They listed them as the use of the Canonical Scriptures and the Creeds, Holy Baptism, Confirmation, Holy Communion and the Ordinal, but added that there were other features 'which are effective in maintaining the traditional doctrinal emphasis and ecclesiastical culture of Anglicanism'. These were spelt out in the Committee report. (ibid, pp.280-281)

The 1968 Conference resolutions made no reference to the Book of Common Prayer but in 1978 the Lambeth Fathers returned to the subject. In Section 2: 'The people of God and ministry' *(The Report of the Lambeth Conference 1978* pp. 76 ff.) they noted again that in the past the Book of Common Prayer had been a unifying factor in Anglican worship. However, the report does not seem to be in any way disturbed by the 'most thoroughgoing revisions of the services in recent years', seeing worship, as a whole, as the important unifying force 'as is evidenced by the remarkable agreement on the structure of the Eucharist that has developed in recent years'. The Section's report believed that a unity in structure can 'co-exist with flexibility in content and variety in cultural expression'. (ibid, p.957)

The same Lambeth Conference asked provincial liturgical committees to keep in touch through the ACC (Resolution 23). The implementation of this, as we understand it, has been patchy. The time now seems ripe to constitute an Anglican Communion Liturgical Commission (a proposal raised as long ago as ACC-1 by the Church of Australia).

We believe that a Commission would be valuable in encouraging the process of liturgical renewal in Provinces that have so far not made much headway. We recognize the importance of continuing pastoral, as well as theological, education in the understanding of liturgy when revision has taken place. And we urge that practical help be given to training potential liturgists who could become resource people in their own Provinces and dioceses. In some Provinces the 'indigenization' of Anglican worship is developing, and it is desirable that contact should be maintained with other Churches in those places as well as with Anglican Provinces in other parts of the world. And we stress the importance of the ecumenical dimension in liturgical revision and renewal.

In proposing a Commission we do not seek to impose a new uniformity. As the ACC-6 report commented: 'liturgical renewal has helped all Anglican Churches to look together with other Churches for a similar basic pattern of eucharistic worship on which variations can be made... The work of liturgical scholarship has helped us to see an undergirding liturgical pattern and structure within which we can enjoy diversity without threatening a basic unity'. We also see a further dimension in establishing such a Commission, which relates to our current discussions on the nature and sources of Authority in our Communion. We refer to the Lambeth 1948 statement: 'this essentially Anglican Authority is reflected in our adherence to episcopacy ... and the Book of Common Prayer as the standard of our worship. Liturgy, in the sense of the offering and ordering of the public worship of God, is the crucible in which these elements of authority are fused and unified in the fellowship and power of the Holy Spirit. It is the living and ascended Christ present in the worshipping congregation who is the meaning and unity of the whole Church. He presents it to the Father, and sends it out on its mission'.

Professor Lash in his presentation to the Council alluded to the classic 1948 statement and commented that something more is required than an indication of where (such) truth might be learnt, of how it was *once* held, and of the context in which it *would* be held today if only we could find out how to do it. And he raised the question as to whether or not the Churches of the Anglican Communion can co-exist without becoming a *Confessing* Communion of Churches.

Yet our Communion is notoriously shy of issuing doctrinal or confessional statements, while the ethos of Anglicanism has been greatly influenced by the common liturgical tradition and teaching of the Book of Common Prayer. However that book too is becoming a centre which was *once* held. Its influence is waning, though a recognisably Anglican worshipping character persists. Yet this needs to be consciously sustained, expressed, renewed and re-expressed. And we believe that an Anglican Communion

Liturgical Commission could be a very valuable instrument in this process. Moreover, as paragraph 60 in *For the Sake of the Kingdom* reminds us: 'The Church's liturgy carries the common mind of the community, and it is this "mind" with its characteristic questions, interests and assumptions, that receives, and in receiving interprets, the Bible and the creeds'.

An Anglican Communion Liturgical Commission in addition to the tasks delineated above, could, we believe, become a useful means by which the Communion assimilates and expresses its coherence, self-understanding, and vocation within the one, holy, catholic and apostolic Church.

Resolution 12:   Anglican Communion Liturgical Commission

THAT this Council:

invites the Standing Committee to establish an Anglican Communion Liturgical Commission with the following terms of reference:

(a)   to keep under review liturgical revision in the Anglican Communion, both among those Provinces which have gone a long way in this direction and those who have not;

(b)   to offer encouragement, support and advice to those Provinces which have, as yet, few liturgically-trained specialists, whether in the pastoral or the more theological aspects of liturgy, and in some instances finance the training of liturgists;

(c)   to study and reflect on those areas in which inculturation and contextualisation of Anglican worship is developing, maintaining contact with other Churches in those places as well as Anglican Provinces in other parts of the world;

(d)   to study and evaluate ecumenical liturgical developments as they relate to the Anglican tradition;

(e)   and, in doing all this, to attempt to discern liturgical features and principles in which, as the future unfolds, the Anglican Communion could recognise its continuing identity and encourage fellowship with other Christian Communions.

NB   The cost of the commission is estimated to be £8,000 per annum on the assumption that it will meet every two years and have a membership of less than the Inter-Anglican Theological and Doctrinal Commission (15 members).

APPENDIX TO SECTION II – DOGMATIC AND PASTORAL AFFAIRS

A STUDY GUIDE TO 'FOR THE SAKE OF THE KINGDOM'

INTRODUCTION (Chapter 1)

Theme:

The Anglican Church, which was once closely identified with British culture, is now located in many different countries. The report tries to look at the relationship between the Christian Gospel and the variety of cultures in which it is now preached. The report considers this within the wider question of the relationship between our experience of the Church and God's Kingdom as it is anticipated in this world.

Example:

Three friends trained together at college. One went to serve the Church in South America, another in India and the third stayed at home in England as a University chaplain. Many years later they met up again and discussed how their experience of the liberation struggle in South America, Hindu spirituality in India, and Western intellectualism had affected their understanding of the Gospel.

Question:

How would you state the Gospel in your own words?

IDENTIFYING QUESTIONS (Chapter 2)

The report considers some of these questions.

What is meant by the rule, or kingship, or Kingdom of God?
Where and how is it manifested?
Can the saving presence of God – and so the presence of his Kingdom – be discerned in the insights and teachings of non-Christian cultures with the religious traditions or ways of life which they embody?

Can the Kingdom be identified in social and political movements which arise without reference to the Church and sometimes in conflict with it?'

What is your answer to these questions?

BELONGING AND NOT BELONGING (Chapter 3)

Theme:

Every Church is set in its own soil. It is moulded and shaped by the culture, tradition, customs, economy and politics of the land in which it lives. Yet at the same time it has the opportunity to shape and mould the culture of that land. Even if it is small.

So the Church both belongs, and does not belong, to the land and the culture of that land, in which it is set.

Example

Christians in China look Chinese, speak Chinese, think in forms shaped by the long history of Chinese civilisation and often use Chinese hymns and music in their services. Yet their life is rooted in Christ who belongs to all cultures and cannot be fully expressed by any one.

Question

What are the forces and factors which (a) make the Church belong to a particular culture and (b) which make the Church not belong to that culture?

CHURCH AND KINGDOM IN THE ORDER OF REDEMPTION (Chapter 4)

Theme:

The people of the Old Testament longed for the time when God's rule of love would be established on earth; when all that is wrong would be put right. The message of Jesus was that this time had come. God's kingdom, his rule on earth, was here. After the death of Jesus and his resurrection, the first Christians realised that the promised rule of God had already come in Jesus himself. The Kingdom is spread by those who come to Christ and order their lives according to God's will.

The Church is not just centred on Christ. It is the body of Christ. Through his death, resurrection and coming of his Spirit, Christ makes the kingdom of God present in the Church. The Church is a sacrament and sign of the Kingdom.

Example

In one Church there is a fierce dispute over leadership. The Church threatens to split. However, one of the leaders works for reconciliation and this comes about after people have said 'sorry'. This reconciliation is a sign of God's rule on earth. But the fact that such quarrels are always likely to arise reminds us that God's rule is not yet complete in this life.

Question:

'Thy Kingdom come'. How do you understand and explain this phrase in the light of this chapter?

WORLD AND KINGDOM IN THE ORDER OF CREATION (Chapter 5)

Theme:

We know there is something good in creation because God's Son came to live and die and rise again for us. There is something good in creation itself, because it is made also by God. But human beings have sinned, so the world is alienated from God. Yet still something of his glory can be seen in it. Until God's redemption is complete there will always be a tension between the world as intended and created by God and the world as it is now.

Examples:

A beautiful lake has become polluted by industrial waste. Fish die and the water can no longer be drunk. But still lilies and lotus flowers grow on the lake.

In a refugee camp a mother cradles her starving baby. In her love the glory of God shines out. But the war and famine which have brought them to the camp disclose the sin of humanity.

Question:

Where do you find God's glory most clearly shining out?
Where do you find God's glory most hidden?

GOD'S KINGDOM: A 'YES' AND A 'NO' (Chapter 6)

Theme:

There is that in every culture to which we can say 'yes'.

There is that in every culture which answers to Christ and finds its fulfilment in him.

There is that in every culture which is challenged by Christ.

Question:

Apply these affirmations to the culture in which your Church is set.

PLURALISM AND THE NORM OF CHRISTIAN JUDGEMENT
(Chapter 7)

Theme:

The Church is commissioned to go to all the nations of the world and baptize in the name of the Holy Trinity. Every nation has its own inherited and evolving culture. There is no culture in which the Gospel cannot be implanted and bear fruit.

Example:

The culture is the ground, the Gospel is the seed. The fruit from the seed reflects the nature and quality of the ground. The fruit 'judges' the ground. The ground remains the ground but the seed and its fruit both have a present and a future life – like the kingdom of God.

Question:

Think of your own national culture. In what way do you think that, in comparison with other cultures, it enlarges our understanding of the Gospel? In what way to you think it might offer only a limited view of the Christian faith?

REPENTANCE AND THE VARIETY OF RELIGIOUS CULTURES
(Chapter 8)

A Comparison

The Church is like the United Nations Organisation. Both have an agreed charter. Every independent country finds a place in the UN and renders the organisation something unique and rich because of the contribution which each member state can make for the good of mankind. Yet when faced with disputes between nations, the organisation finds it difficult to carry out its own work and ideals. For it to work, member states have to conform to the principles of the charter. So too the Christian Churches have to conform their life to the fundamental principles of the Gospel.

Questions:

1. What are the fundamental principles of the Gospel?

2. In what way or ways does your Church fall short of these?

REPENTANCE AND MOVEMENTS FOR LIBERATION (Chapter 9)

Theme:

We need to listen especially to those Christians who are materially poor as they struggle for justice. They have insights which enlarge our understanding of the Christian faith and which challenge hidden assumptions in forms of Christianity from prosperous countries. Furthermore, their struggle for full human dignity is a sign of God's active presence, and so his rule, in the world.

Various 'Liberation Theologies' have arisen out of the struggles of the poor. These remind us that God is concerned with the social as well as the individual dimension of our lives and that he has a special love of the poor.

God's kingdom can never be identified with any particular social or political system. But as we struggle for justice in the social order God is actively present anticipating the full realisation of his kingdom.

Example:

Dr Allan Boesak and some others were arrested after a demonstration in South Africa and found themselves in prison in the same cell. All they had between them was one bar of chocolate and one sandwich. They broke these into pieces and shared them round, with prayer and blessing. It seemed to them like a service of Holy Communion.

Question:

Who are the poor in your society and in what way is the Church in solidarity with them?

THE CHURCH AND THE MYSTERY OF GOD'S KINGDOM (Chapter 10)

Theme:

The Church is always located in a particular time and place. Therefore a variety of Christian style and language is entirely proper. However the Church lives in and for the Kingdom of God. Within all the variety it looks for unity in its common loyalty to the Kingdom.

For Anglicans this unity and diversity is focused in the Anglican Communion where controversial issues can be discussed in fellowship.

There is good in variety, for each part of the Church brings something to the whole. There is also good in dialogue. For this reminds us that no part of the whole has all the truth.

Example:

An Anglican group meeting together heard about the millions of abandoned children in Brazil and about the huge foreign debt of that country, so that each child is born $1000 in debt to other countries. All members of the group felt challenged by this.

Question:

Which group of Christians do you feel you need to listen to in order to have your understanding of the Gospel challenged and enlarged?

Section III   Ecumenical Relations

A. ONE LORD

Behind the altar-table of the Chapel in which the Council daily proclaimed and celebrated Christ as the Word of God and the Bread of Life were written Chinese characters: one Lord, one Faith, one Baptism. The Section

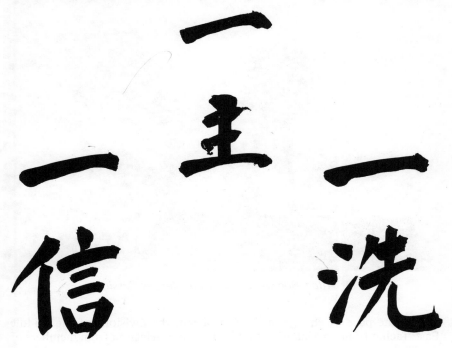

assigned to Ecumenical Relations set their reflection, debate and decisions against the background of these great themes of the fourth chapter of St Paul's letter to the Ephesians. Our unity under the one Lordship of Christ must ultimately become that 'mature humanity', that 'measure of the stature of the fullness of Christ' of which St Paul speaks (Eph. 4.13). The ultimate goal of unity is nothing less than the unity of humanity and all redeemed creation. To rest content with an ecumenism of theological word-games or ecclesiastical joinery is to sell the ecumenical movement short. It would be to confuse the Church and Kingdom and to forget that the High Priestly Prayer of Jesus was 'that they may all be one ... so that the world may believe' (John 17.21).

Dr Allan Boesak and Professor Nicholas Lash powerfully reminded the Council of this in their very different presentations. In the stories members told each other about unity – or the lack of it – we were reminded time and time again of the wider human background to particular ecumenical relationships: the problem of holding together ecumenical leadership and communal sentiment in Northern Ireland; unity in mission in Pakistan and

Dr Allan Boesak addresses a Plenary Session

India;. the pace of change in the Caribbean; the divisions of the Middle East; facing Islam in Malawi – to take a random selection from members of the Unity Section.

Christian unity may not be considered apart from the unity, redemption, and reconciliation of the whole human race. For the Church exists not for itself but for others. It exists for the sake of the Kingdom of which it is herald and foretaste, instrument, sign and sacrament – to use the language found in Anglican conversations with all our ecumenical partners. Because the Church must never forget that the Kingdom comes first, the ecumenical endeavour must always begin with a divided and suffering world. As Professor Lash put it: 'It is only where people actually bleed and weep that their wounds can be bound up and their tears wiped away'. To start here is to see the one Lordship of Christ as potentially encompassing the whole creation.

B. ONE FAITH

Only against such a background is it right to move to Christian unity in its narrower institutional sense. It is indeed the wider context which actually justifies the ecumenical movement. If the Church is to be a sign of God's Kingdom, what signal is sent by a divided Christianity? Disunity impairs mission and flaws the power of the Church to exhibit Christ's reign of justice, peace and love. So, the frail mechanisms of theological dialogue and unity negotiations have their place. They are necessary instruments, of value not in themselves but for their purpose – to enable Christians to be so reconciled among themselves that the Church can more effectively be the proclamation of the Gospel of reconciliation to the wider world.

THEOLOGICAL DIALOGUES

The Anglican Consultative Council has a special responsibility for the theological and doctrinal discussions between Anglicans and other Christian families at the international level. Our ecumenical dialogues are part of the Council's stewardship on behalf of the Communion and they take a significant proportion of its budget. The Agreed Statements produced by such dialogues are by no means the whole of the ecumenical story; but they are an indispensable part of our search for unity in truth. The remarkable convergence expressed in the many ecumenical texts is evidence that consensus in faith is achievable in fact as well as in dream. They count against the contention that agreement in faith is neither desirable nor possible. They provide a common framework of understanding within which separate Christian stories can be owned by others. They provide a gloss on confessional documents which enable Christians of one Communion to recognize the faith of Christians with a rival communal history.

But Agreed Statements are necessarily technical documents. They often deal with the detail of long past controversy in a way which has no immediate relevance to the same Christian communities today. Their assimilation and reception by the whole Church is therefore not easy. The problem is compounded by difficulties of translation and transposition into languages and cultures radically different from that of the original disputes; different too from the necessarily academic forums of international ecumenical commissions.

Such difficulties become more acute when Churches in dialogue are asked to state whether the resulting Agreed Statements are in accord with the faith of their Church – as has been the case with *Baptism, Eucharist and Ministry* of the Faith and Order Commission of the WCC (BEM) and the *Final Report* of the Anglican/Roman Catholic International Commission

Many Gifts, One Spirit

(ARCIC I). But such an evaluation, however difficult, is a necessary part of the search for unity if a changed official relationship between Churches is to be achieved, grounded in agreement in faith.

At the Newcastle Meeting of the Anglican Consultative Council (ACC-5) very careful attention was given to the problem of how the Anglican Communion as such could recognize its faith in ecumenical agreements (pp 39-41 and 43-44). While the Council recognized that juridical acceptance – or rejection – must take place at the level of the Provinces, it also looked forward 'to the Lambeth Conference of 1988 pronouncing the consensus of the Communion'. The Council therefore invited the Provinces to respond to the ARCIC *Final Report* in time for the next Lambeth Conference. It recognized that such ecumenical decision-making posed important internal questions to the Communion: who speaks for the Anglican Communion and how?

The following meeting of the Council at Badagry, Nigeria (ACC-6) gave further thought to this process. It recommended that the responses of the Provinces should be collated in preparation both for this meeting of the Council and for the Lambeth Conference of 1988 (pp 95-97 and 102).

In accordance with this request an ecumenical consultation took place at the Emmaus Retreat Centre, West Wickham, Kent, England from 27th January until 2nd February 1987. The Consultation comprised eight bishops who will be part of the section dealing with ecumenical matters at the Lambeth Conference – including the Chairman and Vice-Chairman – together with a number of ecumenical officers from various parts of the Communion. The resulting *Emmaus Report* was part of the preparatory material for the Ecumenical Section of this Council. It will be published alongside the Report of the Council and reference will be made to its findings in the following review of our inter-Church conversations.

1. BAPTISM, EUCHARIST AND MINISTRY

The Ecumenical Consultation at Emmaus House asked the Council to find ways of eliciting responses to BEM from those Provinces which have not yet replied to the WCC so that a more comprehensive Anglican view might be obtained. It called for assistance to Provinces which have difficulty over the translation, interpretation and dissemination of the BEM text. It also asked what the response to and reception of BEM had to tell Anglicans of their own structures of authority and decision-making.

The difficulties facing many Provinces in responding to ecumenical statements has already been noted. The Council suggests that an enquiry be made to Provinces which have not been able to reply asking the reasons for

86

their delay. When this information has been collated we suggest a staff consultation with the Faith and Order Secretariat to see what resources for translation and interpretation are already available from the WCC and which could be more widely known and used in Anglican Provinces.

The Council also welcomes *The Emmaus Report*'s suggestion of reflection on particular issues raised by Provincial Responses to BEM, namely: Scripture and Tradition; mutual recognition of baptism; the consequences of convergence on eucharistic doctrine and the ordained ministry; the development of personal, collegial and synodical forms of ministry at all levels of the Churches' life; and the relation of the sacraments to division in the human community. (See *The Emmaus Report* 'The Response of the Anglican Communion to *Baptism, Eucharist and Ministry*')

2. ANGLICAN-LUTHERAN DIALOGUE

Relations between Anglicans and Lutherans have developed dramatically in recent years in many parts of the world. The Council welcomes the documenting of this in *The Emmaus Report*. The Council also endorses the *Emmaus* proposals that the Lambeth Conference should commend appropriate forms of 'interim eucharistic sharing' with Lutheran Churches along the lines of the agreement in the USA, or as proposed in Europe.

The Emmaus Report also calls for a study of the goal of full communion and notes the tension between the demands of full communion and the autonomy proper to a Province or world communion. The Council welcomes the Anglican-Lutheran consultation on *episcopé* planned for September 1987, which we hope will go some way to resolve the remaining doctrinal obstacles which hinder closer sacramental relations between Anglicans and Lutherans.

3. ANGLICAN-ORIENTAL ORTHODOX FORUM

These Churches comprise the Armenian, Syrian, Coptic and Ethiopian Orthodox Churches. There are growing communities of Oriental Orthodox Churches especially in Europe, North America and Australia. Anglicans have helped these communities establish churches in their new homes. These Churches are little known, but renewed interest has resulted in the preparation of a book of essays which is to be published later this year by the Anglican Book Centre, Toronto, under the title of *Light from the East*. *The Emmaus Report* also documents the long history of Anglican contacts with the Oriental Orthodox (Anglican/Oriental Orthodox Relations).

A meeting between the Archbishop of Canterbury and the representatives of these Churches at the Vancouver Assembly of the WCC in 1983 recommended a meeting between Anglicans and representatives appointed by the Oriental Orthodox Patriarchs. This meeting took place at St Albans, England in October 1985. Its recommendations included:

(a)   The offering of theological scholarships to enable post-graduate study by Oriental Orthodox Students who have completed their basic training in their own Churches. Equally Anglican students should be encouraged to spend time in Oriental Orthodox seminaries and monasteries.

(b)   Theological seminaries of the Oriental Orthodox Churches could be assisted in the building up of libraries.

(c)   The need for regional co-ordinating bodies to promote understanding and co-operation in areas such as North America, Australia and the UK.

(d)   The possibility of co-operation in the pastoral sphere should be actively pursued.

(e)   The possibility of a joint theological commission should be explored.

With one exception, the Heads of Churches concerned have now responded officially to the report of the meeting. Those who have replied have done so in a warm and positive manner. The recommendations of this meeting are being monitored by a small group meeting regularly in London, England.

Provinces, especially in the areas mentioned above, are requested to review relations between their respective communities and to consider ways of developing them in the pastoral sphere and by an exchange of students.

4.   ANGLICAN-ORTHODOX DIALOGUE

The Council welcomes the full survey of Anglican-Orthodox dialogue contained in *The Emmaus Report*. The Council warmly welcomes the positive assessment of the *Moscow* and *Dublin* Agreed Statements made by the Pan-Orthodox Preparatory Conference in February 1986. It also notes that the Conference recorded an Anglican tendency to minimise the importance of the dialogue with the Orthodox.

While it is the case that a number of Anglican Provinces have few or no Orthodox in or alongside their territories and that for them the dialogue with the Orthodox cannot be of immediate pastoral relevance, the Council wishes to emphasize very strongly that the Churches of the Anglican Communion do not regard one dialogue as more important than another as the search for unity is one and indivisible. Anglicans recognize the hurt felt by Orthodox at the ordination of women. On both sides there is the realistic admission that unity is not to be quickly or cheaply achieved and that both partners must accept each other as they are. Yet, on the Anglican side, there is no wish or intention to demote the quest for Anglican-Orthodox unity to the mere exchange of theological viewpoints or pastoral co-operation.

This seriousness of intent entails the reception of the existing Anglican-Orthodox Agreed Statements of 1976 and 1984 by the Provinces of the Anglican Communion – especially those where significant numbers of Orthodox are found alongside Anglicans: Australia, Canada, England, the Middle East, and the USA.

A perennial issue between the Orthodox and Western Christians is the unauthorized Western addition of the *Filioque* clause to the Nicene Creed. At Newcastle ACC-5 asked that the matter be brought before the next Lambeth Conference, which *The Emmaus Report* accordingly does. But we suggest that there is a need for a brief paper outlining the history of this Western addition to the Creed and reasons for its deletion from contemporary Anglican eucharistic liturgies so that the Lambeth Conference and the Provinces can consider its omission without fear of being unscriptural, of denying their Western tradition or of denying a legitimate diversity in Trinitarian theology. Consultation will also be desirable with other Western Churches.

The Council warmly welcomes the proposed visit of His All-Holiness the Oecumenical Patriarch to the Archbishop of Canterbury in December 1987 and hopes this historic and symbolic visit will further closer relations between Anglicans and Orthodox not only in England but wherever Anglicans and Orthodox are together.

5. ANGLICAN-REFORMED DIALOGUE

Resolution 30 of ACC-6 requested a response to three questions from the Anglican-Reformed Report *God's Reign and Our Unity*. To date three responses have been received. We now repeat the questions and invite the Provinces to make their response.

(a) To what extent does the Report's description of the Church as

existing under grace
being ordered for mission in the world, and
being a sign and instrument of human unity
restored in the Reign of God

help you understand Christian Unity in a new way and help to overcome obstacles which prevent Anglican/Reformed unity in your area?

(b) To what extent do the suggestions for ministry in the Report help the search for unity between Anglican and Reformed Churches in your area?

The ACC Chairman (Archdeacon Yong Ping Chung) and the Director of the Anglican Centre in Rome (the Revd Canon Howard Root) with His Holiness Pope John Paul II

(c)   What actions do you intend to take in response to recommendations 1-8 of the Report?

There is a further analysis of the Report in *The Emmaus Report*. The Anglican-Reformed Report is much quoted in other ecumenical documents and has been widely welcomed. It has been profitably discussed by parish groups and now that the programme due to ARCIC and BEM has been largely completed, we once again draw the attention of the Provinces to this useful Report.

6.   ANGLICAN-ROMAN CATHOLIC DIALOGUE

Along with the *Baptism, Eucharist and Ministry* text, the Final Report of ARCIC I has provoked considerable debate within the Anglican Communion. *The Emmaus Report* tells the story of Anglican/Roman Catholic conversations since 1968, the response of the Lambeth Conference 1978, and the responses of successive meetings of the ACC – especially that of 1981 (ACC-5) which suggested the procedure for the evaluation of the *Final Report* by the Lambeth Conference 1988. *The Emmaus Report* collates the responses of the 19 Provinces which have so far replied. It also analyses particular questions raised by the Provinces on eucharistic doctrine, the ordained ministry and authority.

Both Communions are evaluating the work of ARCIC I to test whether there is an authentic agreement in faith sufficient for the next step towards the reconciliation of ministeries. The Council welcomes the letter of Cardinal Johannes Willebrands to the Co-Chairmen of the new Anglican-Roman Catholic International Commission (ARCIC II) setting out possible grounds for this hope. In the meanwhile the Commission has produced its first Agreed Statement: *Salvation and the Church*. The Council warmly welcomes this Statement dealing with the question of Justification by Faith requested by the Council in 1981. In commending it to the Churches of the Communion the Council hopes that some Provinces may be able to make at least a provisional response in time for the Lambeth Conference 1988.

The Council also notes with satisfaction the increasingly important annual 'Informal Talks' between Anglican and Roman Catholic ecumenical staff sponsored by the Secretary of the Vatican Secretariat for Promoting Christian Unity and the Secretary General of the ACC. Mutual trust and candid friendship are a necessary precondition for dialogue and pastoral collaboration at all ecumenical levels.

C. ONE BAPTISM

1. UNITY AND DIVERSITY

One baptism but many Churches. Yet the Epistle to the Ephesians speaks not of many Churches but of many gifts for the building up of the one Body of Christ. This suggests that diversity is not only compatible with unity but actually integral to it. The present meeting of the ACC has been much concerned with the question of unity in diversity, not least within the Anglican Communion itself as it debates matters such as the ordination of women to the presbyterate and episcopate. Both Anglican and ecumenical agendas converge on the question of the unity we seek: a theme developed by all three speakers who addressed the Council.

The Emmaus Report looks at past Anglican statements on this question, especially those from Lambeth Conferences, and finds a remarkable, though far from static, consistency. Unity is a given reality. The unity we seek exists in the unity of the Trinity itself. But it requires to be made organic and visible. The vision of unity does not belittle the distinctive gifts of the separated Churches, and differentiation has positive value. But this value can only be fully realised in a fellowship or communion of one visible society whose members are bound together by a common faith, common sacraments and a common ministry. Here we find the elements of the Chicago-Lambeth Quadrilateral, the centenary of which the Communion celebrates next year.

Though Lambeth Conferences have consistently developed such a vision of unity – the 1920 Encyclical Letter is its classical expression – it has in practice not been so easy to work out what this would actually mean. United Churches have in part expressed the ideal. But no Church other than the former Province of India, Burma, Pakistan and Ceylon has had the courage to consummate proposals for a United Church. Elsewhere, fears of a loss of Anglican identity – among other reasons – have paralysed action. A heightened sense of belonging to the world-wide Church is proper in view of the dangerous rise of nationalisms in the political sphere. But it can be argued that an over-emphasis on international denominational structure or international dialogues makes national unity schemes more difficult. Anglicans must not ignore the undoubted strength and witness of the united Churches in India, Pakistan and Bangladesh. Their unity has meant a mutual sharing of gifts and a new and wider identity.

In his address to the Council Dr Harding Meyer asked whether there is not only a Christian diversity by virtue of the *cultural context* of a particular Church, but also owing to there being *distinct types* of Christianity which all express something of the breadth of the mystery of Christ and the

Church. Should unity take the form of a number of reconciled Churches each very different from each other because they are the Church of that particular place, people, language and culture, or should the pattern rather be of reconciled but continuing and distinct world communions? The answer is not yet known but it is unlikely to be a simple choice between these two models. Our own, limited, Anglican experience of diversity may suggest a pluriform pattern of Christian discipleship. But this would be linked together locally through the office of the bishop and at the wider level by episcopal collegiality, councils and synods. To this some would also add constitutional forms of primacy. We hope that the work done on these issues at the Emmaus consultation will be continued and that Lambeth 1988 will seriously reflect on the emerging patterns of unity.

2.   FULL COMMUNION

Because the goal of unity is as yet unclear the relationship between Churches in full communion also remains imprecise, even confused. This is true *within* the Anglican Communion when dispute or contention threatens the integrity of the fellowship. It is also true *between* the Churches of the Communion and the united Churches and other Churches in full communion with which we have imperfect links and organs of consultation. So discussion arises about inter-Provincial relationships and structures which is both Anglican and ecumenical. Perhaps the primary perspective should be, not 'What should hold Anglicans together?' but 'What should hold Christian Churches together in the bond of the universal Church?' This is indeed the ecumenical perspective of the Lambeth Quadrilateral.

Against this background Anglicans must exercise some caution in defining themselves in such a way that discourages unity proposals. Anglicans have traditionally regarded Anglicanism as a provisional instrument of God's purpose and have not supposed it will exist in perpetuity. The more we stress a distinctive Anglican identity the more opposition there will be to unity proposals on grounds of loss of identity. This problem is discussed in *The Emmaus Report*. Ultimately Anglicans profess belief in the 'One, Holy, Catholic and Apostolic Church' of which we claim to be a part not the whole.

The meaning of full communion has often been debated within the Anglican Communion in recent years. The question is raised afresh for the Church in Wales by the proposals entitled *Ministry in a Uniting Church* of the Covenanted Churches in Wales: would the new Church retain its relationship of full communion with the Churches of the Communion; would it continue to have a place in the international councils of the Communion? Because the Welsh proposals appear to be substantially identical with the

North India scheme, the Council sees no insurmountable problems in relation to the question of full communion.

But if *present* practice is followed, full communion with a united Church does not entail a full sharing in the councils of the Communion. The united Churches of South and North India, and Pakistan send one member each to the ACC. Bangladesh is not represented. Though a larger number of bishops from the united Churches will be attending the Lambeth Conference 1988, they will not have the right to vote. We believe this is less than consistent with being in full communion. We recommend that united Churches in full communion should have normal representation in this Council according to their size. Membership of other Christian world communions should not be seen as an obstacle to membership of the ACC.

The Council also strongly recommends that the Lambeth Conference should consider the appropriateness of united Churches being invited to send their diocesan bishops to the Lambeth Conference as full members. We also hope that the Primates will consider how best to reflect the full communion of the united Churches in the membership of the Primates' Meeting.

We also hope the *Emmaus* working-group at the St Augustine's Seminar will continue to reflect on the meaning of the communion we share with the united Churches and with other Churches: the Old Catholics; the Philippine Independent Church; the Mar Thoma Church. The Bonn Agreement (1931) between Anglicans and Old Catholics officially speaks of inter-communion rather than full communion. What degree of communion do we really share with these Churches and how can we develop these relationships more fully so that they become more truly what they are in name?

3. SYMBOL, STORY AND LOCAL ECUMENISM

In the ecumenical process, we affirm the importance of symbol and story. Symbols have the power to deepen our experience, to open up new areas of meaning for us. So actions and words, opportunities for joint worship and service can expand our understanding of the quest for unity. In ecumenical dialogue, it is important that we have opportunities to tell our own story. We need first of all to tell our story to our fellow Anglicans. Coming to a deeper understanding of who we are enables us to relate more easily to other Churches. Part of the value of meetings of the ACC lies in the experience of sharing our stories, of discovering common stories. We need opportunities to tell our story to our ecumenical partners, to tell them who we are, how we do things and why. We need to tell our own story in such a way that it includes our ecumenical partners. On the local scene, they share the same cultural setting and perhaps some of the same events of our story. And the story continues to develop. Each partner keeps changing and the story is given new twists, new dynamics. Our stories continue to be told but in new ways. The experience of united Churches shows how the common parts of our stories become more important than our separate stories. There is convergence and reconciliation of memories.

There are some necessary elements in the fostering of local ecumenism. There need to be opportunities for telling the story and sensitivity to ensure that stories are heard accurately. Education is a central element in the process. This involves the providing of information in a way that is easily understood locally. This might include the production of simple and clear summaries of the issues involved in major documents, particularly in areas where translation into the local language is not possible. It is important to establish and maintain links between the local and international dialogues so that the two levels of dialogue support and strengthen each other. Above all, encouragement and support for local ecumenical conversations and projects are important factors in fostering dialogue. Local ecumenical projects or co-operating parishes need much support from the wider Church if they are not to feel isolated or frustrated by the structures and institutions of their parent bodies.

In considering unity at the local level the wider goal of human unity is also vitally important. Congregations often first come together to unite on issues of local concern. Local, just as much as international, unity must speak to the wider community. The search for Church unity is sometimes accelerated by external political pressures. There are also divisions within local Churches and congregations which deny the unity of the Body of Christ. Allan Boesak's reminder to the Council of racial division within the Churches in South Africa prompts all the Provinces of the Communion to examine our life for all that makes for division of race, class, education, wealth or gender.

4. NEW CHURCHES AND RELIGIOUS MOVEMENTS

It is paradoxical that an epoch which has been called the Ecumenical Century has also witnessed the greatest increase in Christian division. The growth of new Churches and religious movements has not been taken seriously enough by the traditional Churches. It demands urgent study and response. We are not dealing with a uniform phenomenon or development. It seems to us that independent Churches in Africa (going back to the end of the nineteenth century) are radically different from Pentecostal Churches in Latin America. These are different again from new Churches in Asia or North America. Extensive scientific research on such Churches or movements has not been done.

The Ecumenical Section was grateful for the contribution of its Lutheran Observer, the Revd Dr Jonas Jonson, when it discussed church growth in many parts of the world, including Singapore itself. *The Emmaus Report* lists some of the positive characteristics of new Churches. However a disturbing feature is the tendency of some new Churches to regard unity as impeding Church growth. Another aspect is what appears to be a minimising of the Cross in Christian life. Some Churches exhibit inadequate social concern. Large questions also arise as to the appropriateness of particular forms of Christianity to particular cultures. Are we witnesssing a radically new form of Christianity in these new movements?

Two basic responses are possible towards this phenomenon: renewal within Anglican congregations so that evangelism becomes a higher priority; and a more critical appraisal of some of the characteristics of new Churches. We realise that attitudes may vary towards this kind of Church growth. While recognising the importance of a real commitment to evangelism, the traditional Churches will not wish to undervalue the importance of strengthening a local, integrated, ecumenical, eucharistic community.

Anglicans should be encouraged to attend to the significance of the development of Church growth. Account should be taken of work done by other Churches as, for example, the Roman Catholic document *Sects or New Religious Movements: Pastoral Challenge.*

Resolution 13:   The Emmaus Report

THAT this Council

(a)   expresses its thanks to those bishops and ecumenical officers who drafted *The Emmaus Report* and looks forward to its completion at the St Augustine's Seminar in August 1987 in preparation for the Lambeth Conference 1988;

(b)   requests that the Report be published in study form as a companion booklet to the Report of ACC-7.

Resolution 14:   Anglican-Oriental Orthodox Relations

THAT this Council requests the Secretary General to write to appropriate member Churches on publication of the book *Light from the East* inviting them to consider ways of pastoral co-operation and exchanges of students with the Oriental Orthodox Churches in their regions.

Resolution 15: Dublin Agreed Statement 1984

THAT this Council commends *The Dublin Agreed Statement 1984* of the Anglican/Orthodox Joint Doctrinal Discussions to member Churches for study and evaluation.

Resolution 16: Salvation and the Church

THAT this Council commends the first Agreed Statement of ARCIC-II, *Salvation and the Church,* to member Churches for study and evaluation.

Resolution 17: United Churches in Full Communion

THAT this Council:

(a)   resolves that the ACC should now move towards normal membership of the Council for all united Churches with which the Churches of the Anglican Communion are in full communion (i.e. the Church of South India, the Church of North India, the Church of Pakistan and the Church of Bangladesh);

(b)   requests the Lambeth Conference of 1988 and the Primates' Meeting of 1989 similarly to consider full membership of those bodies for united Churches in full communion.

Resolution 18: New Churches and Religious Movements

THAT this Council requests the Secretary General to inquire whether member Churches are aware of research being pursued in their regions on new Churches and religious movements and to initiate discussion with the World Council of Churches and the Christian World Communions on the desirability of co-operation in this matter.

Section IV   Christianity and the Social Order

INTRODUCTION

The world is divided between the 'haves' and 'have nots', the rich and the poor, the highly developed and the under-developed. Another way of seeing this is the gap between the powerful and the powerless.

Economic, political and military power is wielded today within nations and trans-nationally, often with devastating and destructive effects on people and communities. The exercise of power can, of course, come from lawful authority, but often it is exercised in the interests of a particular nation or race or group of people, who get rich and maintain power at the expense of others.

In the Old Testament, Yahweh uses his power for the greater good of his people, whom he calls upon to observe compassion and justice in their living together. In the New Testament, Jesus turns upside down much contemporary dogma and ethics, substituting the greater law of love, and demonstrating servanthood in a non-authoritarian way. The Resurrection following the cross demonstrates God's power, and the promise of the Spirit is the promise of power to love God, do mercy and act justly.

The Cross, at the heart of the Christian Faith, challenges all earthly rulers and authorities, for all are accountable to God the Creator and Redeemer. The Cross frees the followers of Jesus to challenge governments about the way they govern, especially the way they treat the poor, the powerless and social outcasts.

POWER AND POLITICS

Throughout our discussions in Section IV, we have been faced with the powerful impact of politicisation on the communities and nations in which the Church is called to witness and minister.

It would seem that many political structures at national and international levels are not fully in touch with the needs and aspirations of people today. We noted in particular the tendency of some persons who hold political power and office to concentrate on the perpetuation of power at the expense of serving the genuine needs of people.

The Church has a moral responsibility to call upon governments to be just in their policies and actions. Justice requires that all God's creatures should

99

have fair and equitable relations with one another, together with access to available resources. While the government of a State has a variety of responsibilities, it should always use power in an equitable manner. Its laws should be clear and consistent, and it should see itself as a steward of the nation's resources. It should be faithful to its commitments. When the justice principle is observed, the persons who exercise power do so as servants of the wider community and create a climate in which political rights and responsibilities are respected.

The Church needs to affirm that social cohesion is only possible when those rights and privileges are available without partiality.

Political rights safeguard the ability of citizens to be involved in and to take responsibility for the overall direction of the country's affairs.

Civil rights protect freedoms such as freedom of speech, religion, association, etc.

Social rights include having a legal and social environment which protects and enhances the healthy development of individuals and groups within the society.

The Church should be in the forefront in challenging those who hold political power and office to ensure that these rights are protected and safeguarded at all times. For every right, there is an equal duty. The Church needs always to balance rights with responsibilities; otherwise, satisfying one right may mean denial of another person's right.

A primary motivation in such political and social action by the Church will be our need to follow Christ with the poor and social outcasts in our contemporary world.

INTERNATIONAL DEBT

From the report of the Peace and Justice Network we learned how developing nations live under the burden of huge international debts. These debts severely curtail the chance of self-development and independence.

In reflecting on this we started with the scriptural principle that the Church has always recognised that people should pay their debts. However, as Leviticus 25 makes clear, land belongs to God and in the Jubilee Year all debts were forgotten. This part of the Bible makes clear that, whatever the debt, no person can have everything taken away to pay the debt. You should not bring suffering on another person. For we are called to share the goods of the earth, and not to cause others to acquire debts, especially the poor (Exodus 22.25).

The Church can affirm with the Early Fathers that the goods of the earth are given to humanity as a whole; therefore it is a matter of justice that all people have a right to those goods; they do not belong to any one individual, class or country.

During the 1970s large sums of money became available from funds which became available from OPEC oil producers. This over-supply of funds was channelled to Third World countries, creating large debts which they were and are not able to repay. The loans have become burdensome, and in effect have served to increase the suffering of the poor. Very often these loans passed from one account to another in Western banks, as military regimes fulfilled their own needs to retain power and corrupt regimes lined their own pockets.

More recently, some First World countries such as the United States have fallen into debt because of their own consumer policy.

Many of the recipients of loans and grants were controlled through this period by military juntas or dictators. What then is the moral obligation of the people of today who were not involved in the process of going into debt and who have not even benefited from such loans and grants?

In some Third World countries, a major moral dilemma is posed by the difficulty of choice between not paying the debt or dying. If the debt is paid, people will die because of the very high proportion of the Gross National Product of the country that is needed to service the debt, leaving too little for the requirements of the country. Lending of money has always been seen by the Church as an exercise of power. One of the moral obligations of the lender is to look seriously at the capacity of the borrower both to pay and to service the interest on the debt.

We therefore call on all nations of the world to –

(a) review and suggest policy changes related to the operation of the World Bank and the International Monetary Fund;

(b) identify ways that independent financial institutions can reschedule debts so that terms are more favourable to the debtor, or forgive some debts, especially to Third World countries;

(c) come to an agreement for a strategy for bilateral and multilateral aid, preferably through non-government organisations;

(d) review and reorganise the various international trade agreements such as the General Agreement on Tariffs and Trade.

We call on the Churches to identify with the poor and powerless and to become their advocate in these matters. It is hoped that the Lambeth Conference will address the issue of the international debt from the moral perspective.

Resolution 19: The Poor and Powerless

THAT this Council calls on member churches to-

(a)   act on behalf of the poor and powerless, particularly in the matter of international debt;

(b)   challenge their governments to review issues raised in this report;

(c)   channel questions and issues through any representation the Communion has at the United Nations.

POWER THROUGH TECHNOLOGY

The report of the Family and Community Network brought to our attention the effects on families and communities of the unplanned onrush of technology, particularly in relatively undeveloped parts of the world.

No human being or society should operate without limits or without accountability. No experimentation or application of new discoveries can be dissociated from its adverse effects on the well-being and the future survival of people.

We believe it is a fundamental Christian ethical principle that technology should operate within agreed limits. We do not wish to stop technological progress, but to decide on careful limits.

These limits should be determined only after consultation with the community at large within a country, not just with the scientists involved, nor even the institutions they serve.

Only Governments have the power to conduct such consultation and determine such limits, which should then be implemented by decree, legislation or institutional guidelines which can be enforced and monitored.

Christian institutions such as hospitals may voluntarily add to these limitations out of a special sense of respect for human dignity or out of a special moral code thought to be appropriate for a Christian body in that setting.

The ethics of technology are usually seen as matters for individuals, but in our view they are matters of vital importance for whole communities. For example, the infertility which creates the demand for In Vitro Fertilisation is not just a matter for the applicant couple but for the whole extended family and for the community, because of interaction with public policies on abortion, adoption and population. Another question would be the maintenance of life-support systems.

Technology has introduced progress in health care, personal comfort and production efficiency undreamed of in previous generations. We live longer because of technology; pain and distress are relieved; many other benefits come to all of us.

There are also many people of goodwill and of Christian conviction who work in technology, many of them seeking to overcome disease and to bring progress to under-developed countries. What follows in criticism of the introduction of inappropriate technology does not reflect on the goodwill of many involved.

While it is true that developing countries demand technology, what they generally want is appropriate technology. Western technology when imported can make people dependent. Imported labour also causes economic imbalance in the purchasing power within a community.

In the commercial sector of technology, those who have power tend to be those who benefit most from the development of science and technology. The owners and managers of technology and those who sell their products are mostly interested in financial gain, not necessarily the welfare of the people or the environment. So they put into markets, particularly in Third World countries, products which are not relevant to their economies, or in some cases products which are not acceptable in Western countries. An example is the marketing in Africa of Deprovera as a contraceptive when tests had forced its withdrawal in the U.S.

Resolution 20: Modern Technology

THAT this Council encourages member churches to –

(a)   consider the ethics of modern technology, especially in the biomedical area;

(b)   consider carefully any existing guidelines for public and Christian institutions such as hospitals, and if they do not exist, to help develop them;

(c)   examine ways in which Church and nation where possible might welcome technology which strengthens local community development and which is appropriate to that region and nation, and reject technology which is inappropriate, causes unemployment or other suffering among the people;

Further, this Council requests the Peace and Justice Network and the Family and Community Network to monitor this issue and report to ACC-8.

MEDIA

Mass media have significant impact across the world, accelerated in the last few years by the development of satellites increasing the availability and penetration of common images universally.

In 'Western' countries, the media are increasingly having a destructive effect on family and cultural life. This is because of underlying but unstated values affirming violence, sexism and consumerism as common and legitimate human behaviour.

We observe an obsession on television with violence, which is constantly portrayed as a way of solving problems or exercising power. On advertisements as well as in dramas, women are constantly portrayed as sex objects, despite much criticism of this practice.

Mass media are increasingly controlled and manipulated by a few corporations. This has decreased the selection of news and current affairs available on the world's screens. News is often prejudiced and misleading. This leads to what is virtually 'brainwashing' of millions of people to think in a certain way and to form certain attitudes which are not necessarily right and good. It distorts and leads to disinformation being propagated.

We cannot ignore the influence of such mass media on people of different cultures. In our view, people have a right to receive information which affirms rather than destroys their cultural values.

All of this tends to promote individual desire, ambition and consumption, which then has the inevitable result of breaking down family life and community solidarity. This process is very evident in developing countries which have in the last ten years permitted the broadcasting of Western-originated television programmes. Television tends to reinforce consumerism, to develop passive attitudes to others at home and overseas, and to trivialise war and human need. It fosters individualism and is thus an anti-social phenomenon.

What has been said above relates more to commercial television than to national broadcasting systems such as the BBC. Great benefits flow across the world from television films on such issues as the Ethiopian famine or the South African racial situation. Television can provide access to troubled parts of the world which sensitises and informs the rest of the world.

As Western capitalist media penetrate more and more nations, including those currently closed to them, a kind of universal culture develops which perpetuates a myth of white male superiority, justification of the arms race and the legitimacy of the suppression of minorities by majorities. This whole movement is of very great concern.

Having said all that, we recognise the value in the West of radio and television for fantasy, entertainment and relaxation.

There are four roles for the Church in mass media.

    i.   It can be a critic, as described above, calling for greater accountability to the people, control by government and responsiveness to human needs. In some places the Church refuses as a matter of protest to participate in government controlled media. It also feels it has to support alternative media.

ii. It can also raise consciousness in the general community of the values and dangers of the media, encouraging families and congregations to develop alternative social entertainments and educational opportunities. Where media perform positive and educational functions, the Church can support and promote them.

iii. Where the Church is in a position to exercise opportunities in media, and where it has resources, it should develop skill for production of programmes for mass media. Great opportunities for this exist in many countries, but the Church is not always alive to the opportunity or the priority.

iv. The Church should also fight against censorship, and work for freedom of information. This can involve difficult decisions because, for example, of the need for some forms of government regulation to outlaw pornography, limit portrayal of violence, institute film classifications as a guide to viewing choice, and determine standards for advertising and for children's viewing time. All these matters involve ethical choices, and Christians should be active in their participation in these debates.

Resolution 21: Media

THAT this Council:

(a) gives thanks to God for all the benefits provided to life by modern means of communication;

(b) urges member Churches to make effective use of such media in teaching, evangelism and communication;

(c) noting the danger of passive, unreflective and constant viewing, and the absorption of ideas and values alien to local culture and Christian values, calls on the Churches:

i. to help their members exercise critical discernment (e.g. through Television Awareness Training), in both what is good, informative and entertaining, and in identifying biased political attitudes and news reporting, and assumptions that consumerism is a recipe for happiness;

ii. to engage with the media on the dangers of violence, anti-social behaviour, sexist attitudes and mindless triviality conveyed through some of the programmes;

(d)   urges member Churches to make use of the ACC Communications Network to share information and experience;

(e)   encourages member Churches to examine current media censorship and to work for freedom of information;

(f)   urges all member Churches to fight against pornography, unnecessary portrayal of violence, and open advertising for alcohol and tobacco products in all media.

MILITARISM

Militarism has been defined as 'the tendency of a nation's military apparatus to assume ever-increasing control over the lives and behaviour of its citizens; for military goals and military values increasingly to dominate national culture, education, the media, religion, politics, and the economy at the expense of civilian institutions'.

The Provinces of the Communion have informed the Peace and Justice Network of the extent and effect of militarism, a reality which includes conventional as well as nuclear weapons as a worldwide problem.

Resources which would otherwise be available to meet human need and for development are devoted to the manufacture of weapons and the arms trade; communities are being set in hostility to one another; this in turn serves to fuel violence and conflict which destroy families and their communities, creating refugees, social instability, unemployment and other suffering.

While peace and justice bodies in many Provinces have been opposing this trend, this is not enough. Churches as a whole should be engaging in the crusade against militarism, at the local level through an educational process, and centrally through a critical process of making their views known to governments, whether they are civilian or military.

Resolution 22:   Militarism

THAT this Council

(a)   recommends to member Churches that they

    i.   examine the extent to which the arms trade and militarism, as defined in the report, have become a reality in their region;

    ii.   engage in a strategic educational and public campaign against militarism; and

(b)   requests that the issue of militarism be placed on the Lambeth Conference agenda; and

(c) requests the Peace and Justice Network to monitor this issue and report to ACC-8 with a specific strategy on peacemaking which the Communion might follow.

RACISM

(a) *Power over Peoples*

Every human being is made in the image of God, and therefore all are created equal. Human sinfulness asserts itself when people do not respect this equality before God and claim for men and women superiority over others on the basis of race or colour. Racism is sin. Only God's redeeming grace can change the hearts of those who practise racism. To oppose racism is not only to support social justice. It is also to bring in the kingdom of God into community experience.

(b) *Definition*

Racism is the expression of superiority over others on the basis of race or colour. It shows itself in preference of one set of social and cultural values and economic interests over those of another race. It shows itself in discriminatory and sometimes oppressive laws, institutions and society norms. It can be reinforced by forcing people to seek separate cultural identity, rather than to belong to a nation as a whole.

(c) *Examples*

Racism is a South African woman weeping over her son slaughtered by the police.

Racism is Aboriginal families living in emergency shelters on the edge of Australian cities.

Racism is a Maori family unable to fish at traditional fishing grounds owing to pollution from outflow from factories owned by white people.

Racism is when an Indian family at Keruguya, Kenya, refuses to allow their son to marry an African girl he loves.

(d) *Opportunity for the Church*

Within the Church, races come together in a unique way. Politics and social structures may divide poeple, but the Church is called to unite; for in Christ there is no east or west, no slave or free.

The Church in a multicultural society or in a nation where ethnic or aboriginal minorities, or even large racial groups, suffer discrimination, has a responsibility and an opportunity to demonstrate to the nation the reconciling power of the gospel. It will need to put both financial and human resources into this priority.

Racism can be found within the Church; and sometimes people use religious values to justify it. We must expose this; for racism is always contrary to the teaching of Scripture. Such discrimination can show itself within the Church in hierarchical structures, liturgical language, youth involvement, the role of women and in general terms – in the way power is developed and exercised.

We see community development and social transformation as legitimate goals and expressions for the Church in mission and ministry. This was affirmed at ACC-6 and reaffirmed at the Mission Agencies Conference 1986. Such activities directly assist minority and other oppressed groups.

Resolution 23:   Racism

THAT this Council, believing that the Church must tackle and expose the sin of racism:

(a)   affirms that

    i.   all people are equal because they are made in the image of God;

    ii.   any and all expressions of racism must be deplored and opposed, especially structural racism in legislation, migration, education and social systems; and

(b)   therefore *calls* on member Churches to

    i.   expand their concept of mission and ministry to include community development and social transformation for the benefit of minority and other oppressed groups;

    ii.   support existing ecumenical programmes that work against racism, or to develop their own, as a matter of priority and in solidarity with those who suffer.

Resolution 24:   South Africa

THAT this Council, reaffirming its belief that apartheid is an evil racist system and recognising the injustice and suffering it causes:

(a)   condemns the detention without charge or trial of many people including children in South Africa, isolating them from their families; and further expresses support for those within the country who are protesting at this inhumane action;

(b)   reaffirms its solidarity with all those who are suffering for a just society in South Africa in which the peoples of all races will share on terms of equality the responsibility of government and the full benefits of citizenship;

(c)   encourages its member Churches to –

   i. continue their prayers and support for the peoples of Southern Africa in their struggle for justice and peace;

  ii. press their governments to introduce effective sanctions against the Government of South Africa, until a genuine process of change in political structures is initiated;

 iii. urge business and financial institutions within their jurisdictions to disinvest and disengage from the South African economy;

 iv. ensure that none of their own financial resources is used to support the present regime in South Africa and for this purpose to disinvest from all corporations which have a financial stake in South Africa;

A child at Crossroads squatter camp, South Africa

(d) urges the Government of South Africa to –

    i. bring the present State of Emergency to an end;

    ii. release without delay all political prisoners, including Nelson Mandela;

    iii. release without delay all those who have been detained without trial, especially the children;

    iv. enter into serious negotiation with authentic leaders of all races to prepare a new Constitution;

(e) i. reaffirms resolutions on Namibia passed at ACC-6 expressing the Council's solidarity with the people of Namibia in their struggle for independence and calling on the South African Government to carry out the terms of United Nations Resolution 435;

    ii. further calls on the Provinces of the Communion to report to the Standing Committee of the ACC on action taken on Namibia within their Provinces;

(f) affirms its solidarity with the Front-line States in their efforts to secure a just solution to the problems of South Africa and Namibia and condemns the unprovoked aggression on some Front-line States by the South African Government;

(g) directs the Secretary General to convey to the Archbishop of Cape Town, the Bishop of Namibia, the Secretary of the South African Council of Churches and the Secretary of the Namibian Council of Churches copies of this Resolution together with an assurance of the Council's continued support for them and for those whom they represent at this critical time in the history of Southern Africa.

THE PALESTINE/ISRAEL SITUATION

The Peace and Justice Network just prior to ACC-7 spent time reflecting on the terrible difficulties still being experienced by Christians and by other communities in the Middle East.

Particular notice was given to the Palestine/Israel situation. Section IV recommends the following resolution.

Resolution 25: Palestine/Israel

THAT this Council:

(a) affirms the importance of the Church in the exercise of its prophetic role by standing on the side of the oppressed in their struggle for justice, and by promoting justice, peace and reconciliation for all peoples in the region;

(b)   affirms the existence of the State of Israel and its right to recognised and secure borders, as well as the civic and human rights of all those who live within its borders;

(c)   rejects the interpretation of Holy Scripture which affirms the special place of the present State of Israel in the light of biblical prophecy, finds it detrimental to peace and justice, and damaging to Jews, Christians and Muslims;

(d)   calls attention to the injustice done to the Palestinians in consequence of the creation of the State of Israel, and therefore affirms the right of the Palestinians to determination, including consideration of the possibility of establishment of their own state;

(e)   supports the convening of an international conference over Palestine/Israel under the auspices of the UN and based on all the UN resolutions in relation to this conflict, to which all parties of the conflict be invited including the PLO;

(f)   commits itself to continued prayer for Israelis and Palestinians, for Muslim, Jew and Christian, for the achievement of justice, peace and reconciliation for all.

AIDS

AIDS (Acquired Immune Deficiency Syndrome) has been the subject of publications and statements in many of our Provinces. Infection by this virus is sometimes, but not always, followed by the development of AIDS. The number of deaths is increasing rapidly, although it is impossible to give specific figures, as in some countries these are understated because of national pride or for commercial reasons. At present there is no known cure and no perfect preventative.

This situation, coupled with the possibility that other viruses may be discovered which may have worse consequences, poses special problems for the Churches, falling under the broad headings 'ethical' and 'pastoral'.

The first priority is to limit the spread of the disease. The disease is acquired through body fluids other than saliva – semen to blood, blood to blood, and mother to baby. While the majority of cases in the Western world follow relationships between homosexual males, in other parts of the world for the most part they follow heterosexual relationships. But this pattern is changing. The disease is also transmitted by the needles used in the administration of drugs. The Church, then, should first of all call on all people to exercise personal and communal preventative methods. The Church in each Province must then develop this social ethic as appropriate to their culture and their biblical understanding.

AIDS

Some Guidelines
for Pastoral Care

Published for the Board for Social Responsibility of the Church of England

It is only realistic to accept that there are many who do not uphold the standards set by the Church. They must be urged to take all possible precautions, such as the use of condoms. It cannot be denied that this advocacy of the use of condoms may cause greater promiscuity. In addition, it has been noted that certain firms have seized the opportunity of taking financial advantage by marketing an inferior product.

Next in priority is the need for educational programmes, ideally produced by the State with the support of the Churches, including warnings against the irresponsible use of drugs. Such educational programmes will have to be explicit, and some governments may be inclined to tone them down for fear of causing offence. They should be urged to face the reality of the situation. Governments should also ensure that adequate medical services are available for victims of the disease.

For persons with AIDS and their families, the Church must have a special pastoral concern. While medical science continues to search for a cure, the Churches must help the patients to bear their sufferings and to die with dignity, as in the case of other terminal illnesses. Some Churches have published guidelines for pastoral care of patients and their families, and we would encourage them to allow other Churches to use their publications.

The attitude of the general public varies from indifference to panic. We would discourage both extremes. A person suffering from AIDS should be treated by the community as any other sick person. In accordance with our Lord's command, the victim and his/her family should be supported by the community's prayer and practical help and visits. The precautions which would normally be taken against all infections should also be taken here, it being noted that infection by the AIDS virus cannot occur through normal social contact.

Resolution 26: AIDS

THAT the Council, conscious of the spread of AIDS and the need for a Christian response –

(a) urges all people to examine their life-styles, to uphold fidelity within marriage and chastity outside it; and to refrain from taking illegal drugs;

(b) recommends to the member Churches –

    i. the development of theological and pastoral guidelines on AIDS appropriate to their culture and biblical understanding;

    ii. the sharing of guidelines and information with other Churches through the ACC as members of the Anglican family;

iii. the working with their governments in conducting public educational campaigns, providing medical services, and making
available additional funds for research;

iv. the encouragement of prayer for persons with AIDS, their
families, their friends, and their care-givers and those scientists
engaged in the search for a cure;

(c) requests the Associate Secretary for Mission and Social Issues to
monitor this issue and report to Standing Committee and ACC-8.

WOMEN AND MEN

From the first meeting of the International Family Network, at which 17
Provinces of the Communion were represented, came strong representa-
tions about the role of women and men in our societies.

What became clear, as experiences were shared of family welfare work and
family ministries, was that it is time for the Communion to affirm the role
of women in Church and community life.

Within the community of faith, the dominance of men over women,
sometimes justified on religious grounds, is as much a sin as racism. Since
relations between the sexes are fundamental to the social construction of
reality in all societies, it is critical that we address any oppression which
exists as well as any discrimination within the Church.

1. Poverty

The overriding reality faced by the majority of humanity today is poverty
and malnutrition. The daily task of most humans is survival. It is now
universally recognised that women with dependent children suffer poverty
most. This is called the 'feminisation of poverty'.

2. Work

Work outside the home is usually defined as done by men for wages. The
reality is that women do the same work for much less pay, and still carry the
major household responsibilities. Because of low status and interruptions to
their career, women suffer injustices in the work-place and seldom achieve
positions of responsibility. This applies to the Church as well. Sexual
harassment in the work-place is another hazard women face.

3. Bible Teaching

Biblical passages and Church tradition have been used to justify the fact
that most positions of authority in the Church remain in the hands of men
while women make up the greater proportion of active Anglicans. The
Church is uneasy about addressing this imbalance because of vested interests in maintaining ecclesial order. But both the Bible and today's
churchwomen call for it to be addressed.

The Bible contains both positive and negative stories about relationships
between women and men. There are stories of faithfulness and integrity,
and there are stories of betrayal, incest, murder and hatred. So, domestic
life in its reality is depicted. What the Bible does not do is praise any family
or household type as morally or spiritually superior to the other. What the
Bible does contain are legal and ethical codes protecting human life, con-
trolling abuse of women, justly distributing property, and promoting social
order and fidelity to God.

4. Marriage

While the Church places high value on marriage, we recognize that many
external factors make it difficult for people to fulfil their calling by God to
marriage and family life. Poverty, the search for work away from home and
political forces can all undermine any possibility of solemnizing or realising
marriage. Often, women are left behind to raise the children and maintain
the home while the man is forced, for one reason or another, to find work
elsewhere.

Because of these external factors, together with breakdown in the personal
relationships, marriage breakdown is an increasing reality in all cultures.
Men and women find it increasingly difficult to maintain long-term stable
relationships when there are fewer social supports and when the function of
the relationship is evaluated mainly in terms of emotional satisfaction to the
individual.

Moreover, women are increasingly not prepared to remain in marriages
which have become violent. When marriages break up women usually fall
into poverty and need, and in many nations there are no 'safety nets' provided by a social security or social welfare system.

If the Church is to respond creatively to these issues, it must reassess its
theological and pastoral understanding of marriage, divorce and remar-
riage. It will need to become a stronger advocate for the needs and rights of
women and children in these situations. It will also need to recognise that
marital break-down is seldom caused by 'feminism' but rather by accumula-
tion of injustices and relationship breakdown.

A young black family in South London outside their renovated council flat

The place of sole parents, whether unmarried or once married, is difficult in every culture. The Church needs to welcome these people, who are often socially isolated, and include them in their fellowship.

Any pastoral ministry which emphasizes the family can disenfranchise individuals. If the Church is seen as an extended family, this can include single adults and welcome their gifts.

5. Sexuality

The Church is perceived as having a preoccupation with sex rather than sexuality. This has, at times, led to imbalances in its social teaching, particularly in relation to:

(a) an emphasis on sexual ethics rather than sexual theology.

(b) an emphasis on conscience to the exclusion of responsible freedom, for example in the issue of abortion.

(c) an emphasis on law to the exclusion of grace.

(d) a preoccupation with the biological basis of sex to the exclusion of the social context.

(e) a separation of body matter from spirituality and salvation.

(f) a spiritual dichotomy whereby males have 'masculine attitudes' and females have 'feminine attitudes'.

(g) an emphasis on genital sex rather than a more holistic expression of sexuality which can have meaning for the majority of human beings including children, the elderly, and the physically and mentally disabled.

(h) a concern to protect the sexual property rights of men over and against women. This has been in part demonstrated by the slowness of the Church (and indeed society at large) to recognise the rights of women in the domestic sphere and within marriage.

These imbalances in perspective have important implications for the Church's commitment to openness and inclusiveness. Dealing with such issues can cause deep pain.

6. Violence

In many cultures the brokenness between the sexes is evident in wife-battering and child abuse. This is not just a phenomenon of developed countries. People commonly take out their frustration or inability to develop satisfactory relationships on those closest to them. If in their society there is an ideology of male dominance, this is used to justify the violence. Again, it is the women and children who suffer.

The Church has been taking up the challenge to operate welfare programmes to support and protect these people. But more is needed; the Church needs to confront prophetically the phenomenon of male violence and make sure its teachings cannot be construed to justify it.

7. Fathering

The Church needs to affirm that parenting is a calling and a vocation given to *both* fathers and mothers. The raising, care and teaching of children is not just 'women's work'. We must face head-on the serious situation of the abdication of men in modern societies from fatherhood. In some cultures, women bear children and exclude the fathers from child-raising. The Church in those areas must address this.

Since children learn by observing, both parents need to provide models of tenderness and care-giving, and the Church should be encouraging this. Otherwise, we will raise generations unable to be fully human.

Resolution 27:   Family and Community

THAT this Council:

(a) affirms:-

    i.   the equality of women and men before God and in the exercise of the gifts God has given them, including leadership in the Church;

    ii. the significant role both parents should have in the care and raising of children;

    iii. that, while marriage and family are important ideals for the Church to uphold, single people have much to contribute to the life of the Church, which can become an extended family or 'open community', welcoming everybody.

(b) calls on member Churches to:-

    i.   investigate the suffering of women and men in their region because of poverty, marriage breakdown, economic and political forces and structural discrimination;

    ii. develop appropriate welfare programmes and ministries to families and communities which promote social justice as an expression of the gospel;

    iii. reassess, in co-operation with other Christian Churches, their theological and pastoral understanding of marriage, widowhood, divorce, remarriage and singleness, so that the needs of the disadvantaged get priority;

    iv. examine the extent of domestic violence in their region and develop reconciling and caring ministries to assist, ensuring that no Church teaching can be used to justify such violence;

    v. examine how pornography and prostitution exploit women and children in their region, for the tourist trade and other purposes;

    vi. where possible and culturally appropriate work towards inclusive language in liturgy and church publications;

(c)   requests the Secretary General to send copies of this resolution to the World Council of Churches and other ecumenical partners, and to request the Family and Community Network to monitor these issues and report further to ACC-8.

ENVIRONMENT

The section on Christianity and Social Order had a full discussion on the topic of the Environment. This discussion was introduced by a paper forwarded by the Church of Ireland. This discussion touched on three main areas of concern.

1. *Environmental Accidents* The Section took note of a number of environmental accidents with loss of lives during the past two years – Bhopal gas emission, Chernobyl nuclear explosion, and the many shipping accidents which have polluted shores and oceans.

2. *Industrial Pollution* The Section discussed the growing catalogue of problems which have resulted from industrialisation in both developed and developing countries: polluted rivers, acid rain, airborne lead. Too rapid development in some countries has destroyed traditional lands and upset rural and urban ecology.

3. *Development Issues* The Section took note of the many manifestations of environmental problems in poor countries: soil erosion, deforestation and desertification. In other cases, the problem is caused by uneconomic agriculture or water pollution.

4. *Nuclear testing in the Pacific* is a particular form of environmental pollution which the churches in the Pacific call into question.

Both data and experience show that the damage to the environment effects everybody. Loss of rain forests will upset the climates not only of tropical countries but could also affect the whole world's climate. Loss of soil in the highlands of one country can being famine and loss of lives and property to that country, with refugees spilling over into a neighbouring country. Many view this as despoilation of the planet in a way from which it may never recover.

Environmental concerns and development are not viewed as being in conflict. Development does not solely mean industrialisation. Nor is environmentalism necessarily anti-progress. Both should have the same goal: relieving the pressures on forest, soil and grass, while at the same time bringing progress to society.

The Section welcomed the proposed formation of a Development Network which will be able to monitor these issues.

Resolution 28: The Environment

THAT this Council

(a)   requests the Standing Committee when deciding on future subjects for the Inter-Anglican Theological and Doctrinal Commission to consider a theological study of the understanding of creation in terms of ecology – the wholeness of creation – for circulation and discussion in the Communion;

(b)   requests the Secretary General, through the networks or other sources, to identify and circulate available environmental studies to the Provinces. Of special note is the United Nations Brundtland Report on Environment and Development;

(c)   encourages the member Churches to participate in community development schemes, giving special attention to Section 5 of the report of Mission and Ministry ACC-6 entitled 'Service and Social Transformation';

(d)   calls on member Churches to join with governments where possible in providing the leadership and education to provide appropriate balance between development and environmental issues.

COMMUNITY DEVELOPMENT

Section IV reaffirms the ACC-6 conclusion *(Bonds of Affection,* p. 56) that community development is an aspect of the mission of the Church.

ACC-6 recommended seven principles, which we reaffirm:

(a)   In all programmes we remember that God is already active in the communities we serve.

(b)   Christian funding agencies should not impose their own models of development.

(c)   Diocesan development programmes should become self-supporting.

(d)   Fund-raising must be in accordance with the gospel.

(e)   Agencies and recipients should be careful and accountable stewards.

(f)   Partners in Mission should be used for an annual review process.

(g) Care must be taken not to duplicate community development activities.

The Family and Community Network identifies the possibility of local congregations becoming 'communities of hope' which welcome everyone and which help their local community towards development.

The Anglican Church is faced with increasing numbers of people and communities trying to eke out an existence in extremely difficult 'survival' type situations or in situations where they feel dislocated and despairing. The Family and Community Network shared experiences from many Provinces in the Anglican Communion.

In Hong Kong, the tendency towards nuclear-type family groupings, the movement of families to the New Territories, the government's housing policy that reinforces small families and separates family networks.

In Kenya, in rural villages, land is so important that, because of difficult economic forces, men go off to Nairobi to find short-term work with the aim of returning to the land. Nairobi is already over-populated, with high unemployment. Often the circumstances are so overwhelming that they remain in the city. The result is two-home families and the estrangement of fathers from the rest of their family.

In South Africa, labour-market policies of government split families causing men to work in cities separated by hundreds of miles from families in 'homelands'.

In the Philippines, especially in the rural areas, adverse economic conditions and the break-down of traditional communities mean that the young and fit leave rural areas for work in the cities. Many go overseas to work as maids in Hong Kong, Singapore and wider, or as factory hands, leaving husbands, wives, parents and children in the Philippines.

In Canada, high unemployment due to economic recession places heavy burdens on families. Many break up. Many experience domestic violence, sexual abuse, isolation and poverty. Increasing numbers of lone-parent families headed by women mean that one and a half million women and one million children live below the poverty line.

In Brazil, a nation of 130 million people, people drift to large cities for work, health-care and education.

They find themselves in slum areas on the periphery of cities. Teenage pregnancies (child mortality rates are around 12%), abandoned children who live in poverty, child and youth delinquency are all part of the Brazilian's struggle for survival.

In Australia, indigenous aboriginals are alienated from the rest of society. Government policies discourage pseudo-extended family groupings by their housing policy that disallows more than 5 people not related to one another living together under the same roof. High child mortality, lack of relevant educational facilities, lack of land and housing, alcohol abuse and the abiding failure of whites to understand what aboriginals want as a community add up to almost unsurmountable problems and great despair. Notwithstanding large government funds put into these issues, the problems remain.

The relevance of the Anglican Church to these people and others in similar situations is judged by its practical ministry to them as they are. For its theology to be 'living', it must be rooted in the experiences of those living and existing in a real and changing world.

'Community building' approaches are relevant and effective in many of the above situations. They involve empowering people in their own development; they involve empowering them to decide what forms of family and community they want. There is no one model of 'community building'. Political, economic, social and cultural contexts help determine the type of approach that will evolve over them. There is no 'blueprint' plan for community development.

The Christian goal for such development is social transformation, creating supportive social and personal systems which enable individuals and families to survive, to grow towards God and towards one another, and to enable communities to become welcoming and inclusive.

FUNDAMENTALISM

(a) *Extreme Fundamentalism*

The term 'Fundamentalism' has good and bad implications. There is a positive sense in which the Church quite rightly calls people to the fundamentals of the Christian faith. It is necessary and crucial for the Church to do this from time to time. In fact, in some parts of the world 'fundamentalist' simply means 'evangelical'; in other places, evangelicals would reject this term. But there is an extreme form of fundamentalism which causes spiritual, psychological and social damage in some parts of the world. Section IV shared their experiences and discovered common forms of extremism which in each case was based on using the Bible to justify certain political and economic ends.

While it is important for Christian experience to include an emotional response together with an intellectual response to God, groups which focus on the emotional response depreciate the Christian faith and offer only a partial gospel.

Such groups or individuals have a tendency to be judgmental of those outside them; some focus on the exercise of certain gifts of the Spirit as criteria for true membership in the Christian community.

Some freelance evangelists use a strong emotional appeal and present a dualistic view of the gospel which entirely denies incarnational theology and seeing the gospel in an holistic way.

Such groups frequently use modern media techniques to manipulate people in ways which seriously limit those people's freedom of choice.

Section IV identified from their experience in different regions the following characteristics of this phenomenon:

(a) Having an obsession with a millennial interpretation of eschatology which removes responsibility to transform the present world;

(b) holding the conviction that the gospel does not include social responsibility and political involvement;

(c) identifying particular resistance movements as political expressions of Communism which powerful so-called Christian countries are encouraged to wage war against;

(d) justifying certain political attitudes to the State of Israel and the rights of Palestinians.

Resolution 29: Fundamentalism

THAT this Council:

(a) urges member Churches to study the political, social, psychological and economic implications of fundamentalism as described above;

(b) requests the Lambeth Conference to give a priority to discussion of the issue of fundamentalism.

(b) *Religious Fundamentalism as Political Ideology*

Section IV noted the emergence of varying forms of religious fundamentalism as programmes of political ideology. In some cases, such programmes have influenced State policy. This has happened not only in the Middle East, in Africa and Asia, but also to a certain extent in North America. There have been cases where the pursuit of religious fundamentalism as political ideology has resulted in serious violation of fundamental human rights, including the right to freedom of religious belief, practice and propagation. It is recommended that the Lambeth Conference and ACC-8 take up the questions arising from the growing phenomenon of religious fundamentalism expressed in State ideology.

PASTORAL MINISTRY

Looking at international issues sometimes leaves the Church at Provincial or diocesan level feeling powerless before very large questions.

But, increasingly, international Christian agencies have been addressing these matters. The emergence and growth of the ACC networks also helps to reduce these questions to manageable proportions by the sharing of their stories and experiences.

With this assistance, the Church at diocesan level should now be able to take up international issues, especially those with direct impact on their own country. A pastoral ministry strategy should be devised with some of these characteristics –

i.   based on available data on international trade and the economic order;

ii. including an objective assessment of the local political situation;

iii. building on the skills and resources which the Church has, in relation to their perceived place in national life;

iv. calling on the skills and expertise of Christian lay people engaged professionally in international and national affairs;

v.   firmly based on evangelism and social responsibility as expressions of the mission of the Church;

vi. ensuring that the Church is as willing to serve the community as criticise it;

vii. keeping a priority for ministry to individuals, families and groups identified as social outcasts, the poor and powerless;

viii. ensuring that the Church's human and financial resources follow the local pastoral ministry priorities.

No general model for such pastoral ministry can be laid down at international level. Each Province or diocese must do the planning for themselves. But the renewed Partners in Mission Programme provides an ongoing way for Partners from other Churches to make a positive contribution to reviewing priorities.

RESOLUTIONS FOR LAMBETH CONFERENCE 1988

Many of the issues raised in and for Section IV overlap with the Lambeth Conference agenda.

Archbishops Habgood and Tutu, in their letter on 'Christianity and the Social Order', for Lambeth participants, raised many questions touched on in our discussions.

Among them are (in summary) –

1. How do we judge the rights and responsibilities of minorities and majorities in pluralist societies?
2. How does the church live in solidarity with the poor and powerless?
3. How do we handle deep economic divisions and how do we devise a pastoral response for families and community?
4. How do we support State and family, without disregarding minorities?

All these issues are touched on to some extent in this report. In particular, we highlight these specific resolutions which have arisen under the various topics we have considered.

Resolution 30: Issues for the Lambeth Conference 1988

THAT this Council requests:

(a) the issue of militarism to be placed on the Lambeth Conference agenda;

(b) fundamentalism be given a place on the agenda of the 1988 Lambeth Conference.

MAINTAINING NETWORKS

The experience of establishing and working with the two developed networks – Peace and Justice, and Family and Community – has been both rewarding and fruitful. It has allowed a sharing of experience from across the whole Communion and brought together the rich resources represented by those who have participated on behalf of their Province. Within a remarkable range of cultural, social and political contexts we have discovered a common life, shared experiences and understanding, and have developed deep bonds of fellowship and affection in the ministries to which we belong back home, and which we share in common.

An outcome has been the publication of our shared experience; first in the Peace and Justice discussion paper published in newspaper format in December 1986, and then in the series of consultancy reports and

Occasional Papers from the Family and Community Network. These reports have been rooted in drawing on local experience, and we have found great value in this method of working. Section IV supports the convictions of these two networks that there is great value in inter-Anglican sharing at a grassroots level, and looks to the Council to affirm it. We believe that it represents an excellent way of drawing on expertise already present in the Communion and of allowing different Provinces to speak directly to each other and to the Council on matters of major public concern, so that in each place relevant and informed action can be taken, and so that Social Order questions can be monitored for the Council in an ongoing way.

FUNDING

The Peace and Justice Network started with a seeding grant from a fund within the Episcopal Church of the USA and has been self-funding since. The Family and Community Network has been underwritten by the Mission of St James and St John in Australia and various aspects have been funded by international agencies. In both cases some Provinces financially assisted their representatives to attend the network meeting just prior to ACC-7. The ACC has made no financial contribution to these networks.

Estimated cost of maintaining the two networks are US $25,000 a year for Peace and Justice (including an annual meeting) and US $50,000 a year for Family and Community (including consultancies and regular communications). In both cases, each stage and meeting in the life of the network are self-funding, and proceed only as funding becomes available.

THE ACC OFFICE

Both networks draw their credibility and authenticity from being under the umbrella of the ACC. Both need the affirmation of the Council and the support of ACC staff if they are to continue. Both networks wish to remain specialist networks drawing directly on local skills, and resist any move to bring them into centralised bureaucracies. Section IV supports this view.

There is, however, a need for ACC to provide a co-ordination function to enable the networks to integrate with one another and with other activities of the ACC, and to provide a bedrock of administrative support.

The Peace and Justice Network concluded on 24 April that what was needed was a social order desk at the ACC whose sole task it would be to service the networks, assist in finding resources and provide general back-up. The Family and Community Network did not come to such a clear conclusion, but appealed for back-up, affirmation and support from the ACC office.

These concerns were shared with the ACC Standing Committee on 25 April by the chairpersons and co-ordinators of the two networks.

Section IV suggests that thanks should be expressed to the Episcopal Church of the USA for its seeding grant for the Peace and Justice Network, and to the Mission of St James and St John, Melbourne, for its underwriting of and grant to the Family and Community Project, which has now become the Family and Community Network.

The Section noted that both networks, at their meeting which ended 24 April 1987, determined to maintain themselves on a self-funding basis. The Section noted that Charles Cesaretti and John Gladwin are to continue as co-ordinators of the Peace and Justice Network, and that invitations are being extended to John Rea of Barnardo's Scotland, Alison Webster of the Church of England Board for Social Responsibility and Ian Sparks of the Church of England Children's Society to co-convene the Family and Community Network from January 1988 until ACC-8.

The Section affirmed Peace and Justice and Family and Community as two valuable networks in the inter-Anglican family, and the ACC recommended to the Standing Committee that the Secretary General provide such secretarial and office support as possible, without budget expenditure, during 1987-1990.

This Section also affirms the emerging *Refugee* and *Development Networks,* both of which were referred to the section for comment. How they are to be monitored and co-ordinated is dealt with in the Standing Committee's resolution on the matter.

The Standing Committee has composed its own report on this matter. What is at stake is a new decentralised way for the Communion to work, drawing on grassroots participants in ministries and drawing them together in a communion-sponsored set of networks.

PART 3 – UNITY IN DIVERSITY WITHIN THE ANGLICAN COMMUNION: A WAY FORWARD

This report was prepared by a small working group under the Chairmanship of the Archbishop of Armagh during the meeting of the Council. It was discussed by the Council and the Council agreed unanimously to the recommendations at the end of the report.

A. INTRODUCTION

1.   This is a discussion paper. It does not explore the theological implications of authority, but rather focuses on the way authority is experienced in the Anglican Communion.

2.   By tradition there are four instruments for maintaining the unity in diversity of the Anglican Communion:

The Archbishop of Canterbury
The Lambeth Conference
The Anglican Consultative Council
The Meeting of Primates.

3.   These instruments have a moral authority and may express the common mind of the Communion. The Provinces are centres of ultimate authority for themselves. Individual dioceses share various degrees of authority within their Provinces. Anglican authority is described as being dispersed, as opposed to being centralised.

4.   This means that authority at the international or Communion level is the power to persuade. Therefore, it is not strictly possible to speak of an Anglican Church but rather of an Anglican family of churches with particular instruments to promote and express their untiy.

5.

(a)   While the existing instruments of unity have been adequate in developing and sustaining Anglican cohesiveness, there is emerging an awareness of the need to evaluate and reform them.

(b)   A fundamental reason for this is that increasing diversity within the Communion could threaten its unity.

(c)   Until recently, Anglicans enjoyed a unified ministry, a common prayer book, sacramental agreement and a common credal faith. Each of these factors is in turn being challenged or questioned by the ordination of women, the emergence of indigenous liturgies, new approaches to initiation and theological exploration. Renewal movements and different understandings of the mission of the Church are also challenging Anglican unity.

6. Within the Anglican tradition there has been a creative tension between episcopal authority and synodical authority. The authority of a bishop is two-fold; that which is inherent in the 'office of a bishop' (acting in the apostolic tradition as a personal sign of the Church's continuity and unity and on behalf of the people of God within the body of Christ) and that which is expressed by the 'bishop-in-council'.

7. Current thinking reminds us of the provisional nature of the Church as we move towards that unity which is the will of Christ. The reform of Anglican structures can only be fully justified if they help better to serve Christ's universal mission.

8. The existing four-fold instruments of unity have worked because of the willingness of the constituent Provinces, linked by 'bonds of affection', to make them work and to be a family. It can be said that each Province belongs to the Anglican Communion because 'it wants to'. This principle is expected to continue to govern Anglican understandings of authority.

9. Questions are now being raised about the adequacy of some of the instruments of unity as a sign of the growth and vitality of the Anglican Communion. Just as the structures that promote and preserve Anglican unity have evolved to meet growing needs, so it is to be expected that they should continue to evolve in the future.

10. However, whatever form the process of evolution takes, it is expected that the instruments of unity will continue to be consultative in style and persuasive in terms of authority.

B. THE INSTRUMENTS OF UNITY

1. THE ARCHBISHOP OF CANTERBURY

By tradition and consent the Archbishop of Canterbury is the personal symbol of unity in the Anglican Communion. The office contains within itself the respect and affection of the Anglican Communion.

2. THE LAMBETH CONFERENCE

The Lambeth Conference has provided a consultative forum for each of the dioceses of the Anglican Communion through its bishop.

The Conference has been a valuable meeting to discern and express 'the mind of the churches'. It also recognises the special role and inherent authority bishops have in the Church.

This illustration and the cover design are by Justin Swarbrick

However, there are some indications that the time has come to evaluate its contemporary role. Reasons given include:

(a) Its recommendations have been given diminishing attention over the years (see pp 99 – 100 *Highways and Hedges* by Bishop John Howe).

(b) The growing size of the Lambeth Conference makes it increasingly hard to provide for effective participation and decision making. It is also an unwieldy body to gather and organise.

(c) The heavy cost.

(d) A meeting once every ten years may be insufficient in a rapidly changing world. It is noted of course that Lambeth Conferences may be called at any time and this remains the prerogative of the Archbishop of Canterbury, in consultation with the Primates.

(e) Bishops might meet more regularly, effectively and economically in regions. If we are to have an instrument of authority which is to be effective in a rapidly changing Communion and world, it might need to meet more frequently than every ten years.

While the present forum of the Lambeth Conference expresses the collegial authority of the Bishops, there is no forum to express their role as bishops-in-council. The Lambeth Conference does not allow for the presence of all Bishops; nor any clergy or laity (women as well as men).

3.   THE ANGLICAN CONSULTATIVE COUNCIL

The Anglican Consultative Council (ACC) has provided a more representative forum of the membership of the Anglican churches even though lay membership is minimal.

It has studied and discussed a wide range of issues affecting churches at the local level and has assisted them 'in sustaining Networks for continuing planning and initiative across the world' (Secretary General's ACC-7 Opening Address). It has both assisted local churches to fulfil their mission and preserve their unity with one another and it has served the Church by encouraging ecumenical relationships at all levels.

Here, too, there are some indications that the time has come to evaluate the role and effectiveness of ACC, bearing in mind these factors:

(a) The need for ACC to realise its potential to reflect more closely the pattern of representation on synodical bodies at local and provincial levels.

(b) The current inadequate representation of women and young people.

(c) The value of a more effective instrument to respond to questions of faith and order, social and ecumenical issues and to assist the churches to come to a common mind.

(d) The need for a continuing review of the Networks and consideration of the use which may be made of locally or regionally based workgroups.

(e) The possibility of ACC and Primates' meetings coinciding.

(f) The value of a more representative ACC, strengthening communication to and between Provinces.

(g) The concept of a relatively small council being maintained.

In the light of the foregoing, ACC could become a more significant focus for the consultative process within the Anglican Communion and a more helpful instrument for expressing the mind of the churches.

4. THE PRIMATES' MEETING

The Primates' Meeting provides opportunities for collegiality between those having a special responsibility in individual Provinces and with particular perceptions of the broad issues affecting the whole Communion. These meetings, at regular intervals, are a 'meeting of minds' through which individual provincial concerns can be tested by the collective discussions between elected leaders who will attempt to reach a common mind.

The strengths of the Primates' Meetings are that they:

(a) provide collegial support for the individual Primates;

(b) provide support and an advice resource for the Archbishop of Canterbury in his international role;

(c) act as a continuing sign of the communion of the Provincial churches;

(d) provide effective vehicles of communication to and between Provinces;

(e) respond directly to issues affecting both individual Provinces and the Communion as a whole.

Meetings of Primates could coincide or form an even closer relationship with ACC.

C. A POSSIBLE MODEL FOR THE FUTURE

The four traditional instruments for maintaining the unity in diversity of the Anglican Communion could evolve in the following direction:

1. The continuing role of the Archbishop of Canterbury as the personal symbol of unity within the Communion;

2. Regular Lambeth Conferences might be seen in a new light with the benefit of the experience of regional meetings of Bishops. Such meetings could strengthen the collegiality and the prophetic and teaching roles of the Bishops. There is scope for these meetings to invite Bishops from other regions;

3. An ACC structure which makes good its present shortcomings and allows for continuing development;

4. The continuation of Primates' Meetings with their relationship to ACC being further explored.

In addition it has been suggested that periodically there could be an Anglican Congress with wider representation from the dioceses of the Anglican Communion.

To service all the instruments for maintaining the 'unity in diversity' of the Anglican Communion, there will need to be one adequate and economically effective secretariat.

D. A WAY FORWARD – RECOMMENDATIONS

Because the issues are both important and complex it is imperative that a full investigation and consultative process be undertaken.

Cost factors need to be borne in mind at all stages and any change in structures would be expected to be realistic in terms of what the Communion could afford.

The following recommendations are made:

1. that this paper be referred to Primates and Provincial Secretaries with the request that:

    (a) it be considered as widely as possible at all levels as part of the process of the bishop taking his diocese with him to Lambeth;

    (b) initial responses be sought from General Synods or their Standing Committees, such responses to be submitted to the ACC Secretariat by the end of March 1988;

2. that the responses be collated by the ACC Secretariat and the collation, together with this paper, be submitted to the Lambeth Conference 1988.

3. that subsequent to the Lambeth Conference the Archbishop of Canterbury in consultation with the Secretary General be requested to appoint a small working group to prepare a report for consideration by ACC-8.

(It is recognised that responses from the Provinces prior to Lambeth may only be provisional.)

PART 4 – GENERAL BUSINESS

1. ELECTIONS

The following elections were made by the Council:

VICE-CHAIRMAN

Canon Colin Craston – England

STANDING COMMITTEE

Mr. Edgar Bradley – New Zealand
Mrs. Pamela Chinnis – USA
Archbishop Robin Eames – Ireland
Dr. Julio Lozano – South America

2. FINANCIAL MATTERS

Resolution 31 – Accounts for the Year to 31 December 1986

THAT the audited accounts of the Council for the year ended 31 December 1986 as approved by the Standing Committee and signed on their behalf by the Chairman and Vice-Chairman be and they are hereby adopted by the Council. (See p. 139)

Resolution 32 – Budgets for the Years 1989 and 1990

THAT the draft budgets for the years to 31 December 1989 and 1990 approved by the Standing Committee in the sum of £653,250 and £712,000 be and they are hereby approved by this Council but subject to revision by the Standing Committee should circumstances require. (See pp. 140-141)

Resolution 33 – Contributions from Provinces to the ACC

THAT this Council

(a) urges all members to give priority to the payment of at least the minimum contribution requested to the ACC budget;

(b) recognises that there are certain special circumstances which hinder some Provinces from paying their quota to the ACC budget;

(c) invites each Province to notify the ACC Standing Committee in advance about their special circumstances;

(d)   authorises the Standing Committee to

    i.   enter into dialogue with such Provinces with a view to making appropriate budgetary re-adjustments;

    ii.   to take the necessary steps to remedy such deficiencies in the budget as may occur.

Resolution 34 – Inter-Anglican Budget

THAT this Council requests the Standing Committee and the Archbishop of Canterbury to carry forward the proposals for an Inter-Anglican Budget, which would incorporate the funding needs of the ACC, the Primates' Meeting and the Lambeth Conference and in this process to consult the Provinces. The Council expresses the hope that this budget might be operative with effect from 1 January 1990 and requests the Standing Committee to implement this if the Lambeth Conference agrees.

3.   MR TERRY WAITE, THE ARCHBISHOP OF CANTERBURY'S SECRETARY FOR ANGLICAN COMMUNION AFFAIRS

Resolution 35 – Mr Terry Waite, The Archbishop of Canterbury's Secretary for Anglican Communion Affairs

THAT this Council:

(a)   gives thanks to God for the courageous witness of Terry Waite expressed in his care and concern for the victims of injustice and oppression;

(b)   expresses its appreciation for Terry Waite's devotion to the service of God through the Anglican Communion;

(c)   notes with sadness the suffering of all the people in the Lebanon because of the civil strife which is a symptom of the prevailing tension in the Middle East;

(d)   condemns the detention of innocent people against their will in the Lebanon and other parts of the world;

(e)   encourages the Archbishop of Canterbury in his attempts to ensure the return of Terry Waite;

(f)   sends its love and prayers to Terry and his family.

4.   ANGLICAN CENTRE IN ROME

The last meeting of the ACC asked for a review of the Anglican Centre in Rome. In consultation with the Archbishop of Canterbury the Secretary General invited Professor Henry Chadwick to be chairman and convenor of a small review committee which also included representation from Canada,

A helmeted Syrian soldier armed with a Soviet-made AK-47 assault rifle watches a west Beirut street from his sandbagged position.

Uganda, and the USA. The Council is very grateful for the thorough and detailed Report this produced. Some of its eighteen recommendations are more appropriately considered by the Council of the Centre but the ACC wishes to make clear its full endorsement of the Anglican Centre as 'an important asset with considerable potential' and that 'the Library and Director should be maintained' (Summary of Recommendations 1).

In doing this we wish to express our gratitude to the Director, Canon Howard Root, and also to his wife Celia, for all their work on behalf of the Anglican Communion and Anglican/Roman Catholic reconciliation. Our Roman Catholic observer spoke of the positive value of the Centre as a living and welcome presence of Anglicanism in Rome – a city of pilgrimage which other Christians could also own as well as those in full communion with its bishop.

INCOME AND EXPENDITURE 1986

INCOME

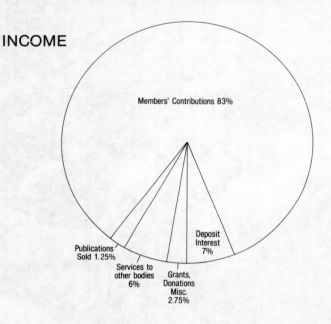

Members' Contributions 83%

Deposit Interest 7%

Publications Sold 1.25%

Services to other bodies 6%

Grants, Donations Misc. 2.75%

EXPENSES

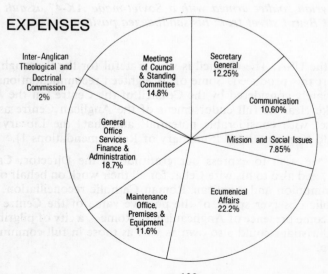

Inter-Anglican Theological and Doctrinal Commission 2%

Meetings of Council & Standing Committee 14.8%

Secretary General 12.25%

Communication 10.60%

General Office Services Finance & Administration 18.7%

Mission and Social Issues 7.85%

Ecumenical Affairs 22.2%

Maintenance Office, Premises & Equipment 11.6%

Summarized Income and Expenditure Account
for the Year Ended 31st December 1986
(Core Budget Only)

INCOME		£
Members' Budget Contributions		424,732
Deposit Interest		35,963
Services to Other Bodies		30,742
Publications sold		6,520
Grants, donations & miscellaneous		13,770
		511,727

EXPENSES		
Central Secretariat:		
Office of Secretary General	62,037	
Communication	53,572	
Mission & Social Issues	39,756	
Ecumenical Affairs (inc Inter-Church Conversations & Rome Centre)	112,542	
General Office Services finance and administration	94,850	
Maintenance of office premises and equipment	58,968	
	421,725	
Meetings of Council and Standing Committee	75,000	
Inter-Anglican Theological and and Doctrinal Commission	10,000	506,725
Transfer to General Reserve		£5,002

NB   The full audited accounts of the ACC are available free of charge from the Secretariat.

Draft Budgets for 1989 and 1990

	1987 ESTIMATED OUTTURN	1988 BUDGET	1989 DRAFT BUDGET	1990 DRAFT BUDGET
Secretary General's Office				
Salaries	50,000	55,000	60,000	66,000
Hospitality	2,450	2,625	2,850	3,150
Travel	10,750	11,500	12,650	14,000
Housing	6,770	7,025	7,350	7,750
	69,970	76,150	82,850	90,900
Communication				
Salaries	35,000	38,000	42,000	46,000
Travel	4,000	4,250	4,750	5,250
Hospitality	275	300	325	350
Publications	25,000	28,000	28,000	28,000
Books, journals etc	1,400	1,500	1,500	1,550
	65,675	72,050	76,575	81,150
Mission & Social Issues				
Salaries etc	33,250	36,250	40,000	44,000
Travel	3,000	3,250	4,750	5,250
Hospitality	150	150	175	200
	36,400	39,650	44,925	49,450
Ecumenical Relations				
Salaries	37,000	41,000	45,000	49,500
Travel	3,000	3,250	3,500	3,750
Hospitality	150	150	150	150
Anglican Centre in Rome	57,585	62,250	68,500	75,000
Inter Church Conversations	40,000	40,000	43,500	46,500
	137,735	146,650	160,650	174,900
Research	–	–	1,500	1,650
General Office, Services finance and administration				
Salaries	72,000	79,000	87,000	95,000
Travel	2,250	2,450	2,700	3,000
Office Expenses	36,000	38,150	42,000	46,000
	110,250	119,600	131,700	144,000

Audit & Other Professional Fees	6,000	6,500	7,250	8,000
Office Rent & Maintenance	41,830	50,000	51,500	53,250
Depreciation on IT Equipt	9,500	12,500	12,500	12,500
Loan Repayment (Ebury Mews)	1,800	1,800	1,800	1,800
Meetings of Council and Standing Committee	60,000	60,000	60,000	60,000
IATDC	10,000	10,000	11,000	12,000
MISAG-2	3,000	3,300	10,000	10,000
Grant to President's Staff	750	750	1,000	1,000
Provision for Contingencies	–	–	–	11,400
	£552,910	£598,950	£653,250	£712,000
(Deficit)	(17,510)	(5,000)	–	–
	£535,400	£593,950	£653,250	£712,000

Draft Budgets for 1989 and 1990

RECEIPTS

	1987 ESTIMATED OUTTURN	1988 BUDGET	1989 DRAFT BUDGET	1990 DRAFT BUDGET
Interests on Deposits	18,000	15,000	17,200	15,000
Received for Services to other Bodies	23,000	25,000	30,000	32,500
Publications Sold	7,000	7,650	8,250	9,000
Grants for IT Equipt	9,500	12,500	12,500	12,500
Special Contribution	12,900	–	–	–
Lambeth Conference a Special Contribution	15,000	20,000	20,000	20,000
	85,400	80,150	87,950	89,000
Contribution from Member Churches	450,000	513,800	565,300	623,000
	£535,400	£593,950	£653,250	£712,000
% Increase in Contributions	7.98%	10.97%	10.02%	10.20%

Note: An increasing amount of work of the Secretariat is on behalf of the Lambeth Conference and Primates Meeting, but it is extremely difficult to quantify this. However, in order to reflect this a total of over £50,000 is included in the Receipts to help to reimburse the ACC for this work. The actual cost is at least this amount.

The Council noted the inevitable tensions which can arise in days of financial stringency when one body (the Anglican Consultative Council) funds an organization and another governs it (the Council of the Anglican Centre).

The ACC also recognized the tension in the Centre Council itself between the representation of the Communion and the management of the Centre.

We recommend a revision of the Constitution of the Anglican Centre (see ACC Handbook pp 20-25) along the lines of the proposals of the Review Committee. However, the members of the Council designated by the ACC should be no more than six. We recommend that where their own Churches are unable to cover their travel expenses provision should be made from the budget of the Anglican Centre and that the contribution by the ACC be increased accordingly. The Secretary General of the Council should no longer be ex-officio Chairman of the Centre Council as this places him in the invidious position of being subject to conflicting loyalties. We note that under the existing Constitution the Secretary General could already designate another Chairman. We recommend that the ACC continues to provide the main part of the Centre budget but would strongly encourage the supplementary funding already begun through the USPG, the SPCK and especially the Friends of the Anglican Centre. We would not wish the Centre to be entirely 'privatised' as it must continue its representative role in Rome. But major sources of income could enable the development of potential through particular projects, increased staff, or the establishment of a capital endowment fund – such as supports the work of the Ecumenical Institute at Strasbourg, with which the Anglican Centre may be able to develop closer ties in the future.

Resolution 36 – Anglican Centre in Rome

THAT this Council:

(a)   expresses its gratitude to Professor Henry Chadwick and his colleagues for the Report of the Review Committee of the Anglican Centre in Rome and accepts its recommendations concerning the revision of the Constitution of the Anglican Centre as modified in the Report of ACC-7;

(b)   further expresses its gratitude to Canon Howard and Mrs Celia Root for all their work on behalf of the Anglican Communion and Anglican/ Roman Catholic reconciliation.

(NB Budget implication: £2,500 per annum from 1988 to cover cost of travel of ACC representatives on the Council of the Anglican Centre in Rome)

5.   VENUE FOR ACC-9

Resolution 37 – Venue for ACC-9

THAT this Council:

1.   welcomes the invitation from the Church of the Province of Southern Africa to hold ACC-9 in Johannesburg, South Africa;

2.   directs the Secretary General to explore an alternative venue in Panama or Central America should conditions be unsuitable in South Africa.

6.   GUIDELINES FOR NETWORKS

From the beginning the Anglican Consultative Council has been charged with the oversight of working groups dealing with issues touching on the lives of member Churches.

The Lambeth Conference of 1968 which set up the ACC also asked that the ACC, in consultation with other Churches, formulate appropriate definitions of terms used in inter-Church relations.

ACC-2 meeting in Dublin in 1973 recommended the Partners in Mission process and Lambeth 1978 encouraged the process.

ACC-5 set up the Mission Issues and Strategy Advisory Group (MISAG-1).

In more recent years, Networks have been formed locally.

Thus, these working groups under the aegis of ACC have tended to fall into three categories:

(a)   Commissions set up by the Lambeth Conference or ACC e.g. the Inter-Anglican Theological and Doctrinal Commission;

(b)   Advisory groups established by either the Lambeth Conference or ACC, e.g. MISAG-1; and

(c)   Networks, which may arise from a particular project, e.g. Family and Community, or because of a special requirement for action around a special need, e.g. Peace and Justice.

At the meeting of the Standing Committee of ACC in Canada in 1986, it was agreed 'that at ACC-7 there should be an opportunity to produce terms of reference for ACC networks'.

Thus it is with Networks we are concerned in this paper.

The Networks were formed mainly on an informal basis. Each has a different pattern to its formation. However, the main purpose of Networks is to provide fellowship, mutual encouragement and sharing of strategy on a common issue. The ACC constitution requires us to develop inter-Anglican communication. After some time people dealing with a subject within the Provinces suggest a meeting after which the sharing and mutual encouragement engendered becomes a bond that results in a request for a more regular gathering. At this stage a Network is born and may take on the important role of advocacy or raising the awareness of the Churches on a particular mission or social issue. Sometimes the Council resolves that a subject be studied within the Communion. This calls for the gathering together of people with experience on the subject and after two or three years a network within the Communion is formed. The ACC Secretariat is in a unique position to co-ordinate the work of all networks. However, it has to be realised that the Secretariat has no executive role except that which has been requested by the Council. The actual management of the various responsibilities belong primarily to the members of a Network.

Where members of a Network have been appointed by their own Churches, and therefore are in positions where they can easily report to the structures, the aspired goals of the Network are achieved. It is to be assumed therefore that the Networks are accountable to the Churches through the ACC for their reports in the same way the ACC is. On the other hand, the Council on behalf of the Churches, can request Networks to look into particular issues or respond to requests from the Churches.

Resolution 38 – Networks

That this Council affirms the value of approved Networks and commissions the Standing Committee to

(a)   appoint a three person working party to consult and to prepare a set of guide-lines for the setting up and operation of Networks

(b)   that the guidelines should include:

i. the requirement that Network names indicate whether they are set up:

1.   by ACC or its Standing Committee;

2.   by another initiative;

ii. the requirement that all Networks have the approval of the Standing Committee before they can be called ACC Networks;

iii. the requirement that the Standing Committee be satisfied as to funding and secretarial support before approval be given;

iv. the requirement that the Standing Committee instruct the carrying out of a periodic review of all Networks;

v. that the involvement of a Province in a Network be subject to the prior approval of the Primate or his nominee;

(c) that the proposed guidelines be:

   i. approved by the Standing Committee

   ii. communicated by the Standing Committee to member Churches together with a list of existing Networks and their status.

7.   INTER-ANGLICAN YOUTH CONFERENCE

ACC-6 Resolution 54 requested the setting up of a Youth Communication Network. Following a meeting of National Anglican Youth officers in November 1985, it had been agreed that there should be an inter-Anglican Youth Conference in Belfast, Northern Ireland in January 1988.

Resolution 39 – Inter-Anglican Youth Conference

THAT this Council

(a)   welcomes the initiative of the Anglican National Youth Officers, in response to ACC-6 Resolution 54 to hold an Inter-Anglican Youth Conference in Belfast in 1988;

(b)   assures the Anglican National Youth Officers of our support and prayers for the Conference.

Patrick and Kieran pictured near Divis flats, Belfast, Northern Ireland.

8. THE PHILIPPINE EPISCOPAL CHURCH – A PROJECTED NEW PROVINCE

Resolution 40 – The Philippine Episcopal Church

THAT this Council

(a) notes that:

  i. it is proposed to establish a new province of the Anglican Church constituted by four dioceses of the Philippine Episcopal Church presently within a province of the Episcopal Church, USA;

  ii. action is being taken in close consultation with the Episcopal Church and with its support and good wishes;

  iii. Bishop R. A. Abellon of the Philippine Episcopal Church, during his attendance at ACC-7, reported to and consulted with ACC representatives relative to the proposed Province;

  iv. the representatives advised the Bishop generally, in particular referred to ACC requirements and guidelines (see ACC-3 pp 59-60 and ACC-4 pp 47-51) and urged that the next draft of the proposed Province's Constitution be submitted to the ACC for comment;

(b) offers the emerging Province the continuing advice and consultancy resource of the ACC;

(c) upon necessary requirements being achieved, looks forward to the proposed Province being a member of the ACC;

(d) encourages the emerging Province and the Philippine Independent Church to develop further their growing partnership with a view to whatever unity seems right to both Churches.

9. CHURCH OF ENGLAND IN SOUTH AFRICA

The history of the relation between the Church of England in South Africa and the Church of the Province of Southern Africa, together with that of its relations with the diocese of Sydney and the Church of England, is long and complex. A Joint Liaison Committee between the CPSA and CESA prompted some hope that reconciliation might be achievable, not least on account of its agreed *Anglican division in South Africa (November 1982)*.

At its last meeting the Council discussed concerns raised by the consecration of Canon Dudley Foord as a bishop in the CESA. Archbishop Donald Robinson of Sydney, who was the chief consecrator, was not able to be present at ACC-6. The section on Ecumenical Relations was grateful for the opportunity to receive additional information and to clarify the issues surrounding the consecration.

Resolution 41 – The Church of England in South Africa

THAT this Council:

(a)   notes that the Archbishop of Sydney consecrated Canon D. Foord on 12th February 1984 on the authority of letters dimissory from the Rt Revd S. C. Bradley;

(b)   further notes a Statement made by the Archbishop of Sydney before the consecration which was a gesture of goodwill and encouragement;

(c)   recognises the Church of the Province of Southern Africa's efforts in seeking reconciliation with the Church of England in South Africa;

(d)   encourages the re-establishment of the Joint Liaison Committee between the Church of the Province of Southern Africa and the Church of England in South Africa and hopes that progress can be reported by the Church of the Province of Southern Africa to ACC-8.

10.   VOTES OF THANKS

Resolution 42 – Votes of Thanks

(a)   Archbishop of Canterbury

THAT this Council gives thanks to the Archbishop of Canterbury for his leadership and inspiration as President of the ACC.

(b)   Chairman of ACC

THAT this Council gives thanks to the Chairman of the ACC, Archdeacon Yong Ping Chung for the able manner in which he presided over its deliberations.

(c)   Outgoing Members

THAT this Council gives thanks to God for the contribution of the following outgoing members who have served it faithfully. This Council assures them of its prayers.

> Bishop Sumio Takatsu – Brazil
> Archbishop Gregory Hla Gyaw – Burma
> Bishop Patrice Njojo – Burundi, Rwanda and Zaire
> The Revd John Makokwe – Burundi, Rwanda and Zaire
> Mrs Patricia Bays – Canada
> Archbishop French Chang-Him – Indian Ocean
> Mr Barry Deane – Ireland
> Mr Ibrahim Wakid – Jerusalem and the Middle East

The Most Revd Brian Davis – New Zealand
The Very Revd Samuel Johnson – Nigeria
The Rt Revd Arne Rudvin – Pakistan
The Revd Gideon Waida – Papua New Guinea
The Rt Revd Lawrence Zulu – Southern Africa
The Rt Revd I Jesudasan – South India
The Most Revd John Ramadhani – Tanzania
The Revd Canon Benezeri Kisembo – Uganda
Professor Enoka Rukare – Uganda
The Very Revd Frederick H. Borsch – USA
The Revd David S. Benjamin – West Indies

and in particular gives thanks for the work of the following members retiring from the Standing Committee:

Mrs Patricia Bays
The Revd Canon Benezeri Kisembo

(d)   THAT this Council expresses its gratitude for the excellence of the Presentation Addresses made by

Professor Nicholas Lash
Dr. Harding Meyer
Dr. Allan Boesak

which did much to stimulate debate on 'The Unity we Seek'.

(e)   Ecumenical Partners

THAT this Council gives thanks to the following Ecumenical Partners for their presence and participation and for their wise counsel and advice

The Revd George Ninan – Christian Conference of Asia
Dr. Jonas Jonson – Lutheran World Federation
The Rt. Revd. Philipose Mar Chrysostom – Mar Thoma
    Syrian Church of Malabar
The Revd. John Chryssavgis – Orthodox Church
The Rt. Revd. Gerhard A. Van Kleef – Old Catholic Church
Fr. Kevin McDonald – Roman Catholic Church
The Revd. Dr. Stephen C. Tan – World Alliance of Reformed
    Churches
Mr. William Thompson – World Council of Churches

(f)   Diocese of Singapore

THAT this Council expresses its appreciation and gratitude to the following:

i. The Right Reverend Dr. Moses Tay, Bishop of Singapore, for the invitation to meet in Singapore and for the hospitality and fellowship of the Diocese;

ii. The Revd. Dr. Louis Tay, Vicar of St. Andrew's Cathedral, for the opportunity to worship in the Cathedral Church;

iii. Mr. George Seow, the Liaison Officer for the Diocese of Singapore;

iv. Mr. Lim Ewe Huat for organising the Opening Service and reception at St. Andrew's Cathedral;

v. The Revd. Canon Frank Lomax for arrangements for worship at the RELC Chapel;

vi. the clergy and people who hosted delegates;

vii. those who offered their time and talents to enable the work of the Council, especially Miss Bessie Lee who played the organ at the morning Eucharist, Miss June Tan as Press Liaison Officer, Miss Chee Mee Lin and Miss Han Ya Ni for secretarial assistance, and Mr. Georgie Ong who was responsible for the reception arrangements for the delegates;

viii. the management and staff of the regional English Language Centre for their co-operation;

ix. Mrs. Marjorie Lau who co-ordinated the making of needlepoint kneelers for each delegate.

(g) Donors

RESOLVED THAT this Council acknowledges with gratitude:

i. the presence and invaluable work of the communicators and in particular expresses its thanks to those Provinces and newspapers which have financed the attendance of communicators;

ii. several Provinces and donors who have made substantial financial contributions to the life and work of the Council and various networks.

(h) Staff and Volunteer Staff

RESOLVED THAT this Council:

i. gives thanks and praise for the leadership, vision and expertise of the Secretary General, the Reverend Canon Samuel Van Culin; and

ii. offers its deepest appreciation and commendation to the staff of the ACC and Lambeth Palace, both to those who remained in London and in particular those in Singapore who have facilitated this seventh meeting of the Council:

The Revd. George B. Braund
Mr. Robert Byers
Mrs. Christine Codner
The Revd Stephen Commins
Miss Flavia Gonsalves
Miss Deirdre E. Hoban
Mr. David J. B. Long
The Revd. Canon Martin Mbwana
Miss Emma Morgan
The Rt. Revd. Michael Nazir-Ali
The Revd. Canon Howard Root
The Revd. Michael C. Sams
The Revd. Canon Roger Symon
Ms Vanessa Wilde;

iii. and extends its appreciation to the Consultants and Section Staff:

The Revd. Charles Cesaretti
The Revd. Richard Harries
The Revd. Canon Christopher Hill
Professor Nicholas Lash
The Rt. Revd. Kenneth Mason
Dr. Harding Meyer
The Ven Alan Nichols
Dr. George Ninan
The Revd. Pritam Santram;

iv. and

notes with praise the presence and ministry of communication staff:

The Revd. John Barton – Chief Broadcasting Officer, Church of England
The Revd. Peter Davis – Director of Communications, Church of the Province of New Zealand
The Revd. Charles Long – Editor of Forward Movement Publications, Cincinnati, ECUSA
Mrs. Ruth Nicastro – Missioner for Communications, Diocese of Los Angeles, USA
Mr. Stephen Webb – Assistant to the Editor, *Church Scene,* Australia
Miss Susan Young, News Editor, *Church Times*, London

i. requests that the Secretary General presents a fair copy of this resolution to those mentioned by name.

PART 5 – PARTICIPANTS IN ACC-7

MEMBERS, PARTICIPANTS AND STAFF

PRESIDENT (ex-officio)
The Most Revd and Rt Hon Robert A. K. Runcie
Archbishop of Canterbury

CHAIRMAN
The Ven. Yong Ping Chung
East Asia

VICE-CHAIRMAN
The Revd Canon Colin Craston
England

SECRETARY GENERAL
The Revd Canon Samuel Van Culin
Anglican Consultative Council

MEMBERS

In the list which follows, members of the Standing Committee whose term of office ended at ACC-7 are indicated by the sign (*), members of the Standing Committee whose term of office began at the end of ACC-7 are indicated by the sign (#), and members of the Standing Committee who served both before, during and after ACC-7 are indicated by both (*#).

The Section to which a member was assigned is given after each name, and section chairmen are shown by the letter C after the section number.

The final column gives the meeting of the ACC after which the member's term of appointment ends.

Australia	The Most Revd Donald Robinson Archbishop of Sydney	2	ACC-9
	The Ven Ian G George	4	ACC-8
	Mr Max F Horton	1	ACC-8

Brazil	The Rt Revd Sumio Takatsu Bishop of South Central Brazil	1	ACC-7
Burma	The Most Revd Gregory Hla Gyaw Bishop of Rangoon and Archbishop of Burma (was unable to attend)	1	ACC-7
Burundi, Rwanda and Zaire	The Most Revd Justin Ndandali Bishop of Butare and Archbishop of Burundi, Rwanda and Zaire (replaced at 1987 meeting by The Rt Revd Patrice Njojo Bishop of Boga-Zaire)	1	ACC-7
	The Revd John W Makokwe	2	ACC-7
Canada	The Most Revd Douglas Hambidge Archbishop of New Westminster	1	ACC-9
	The Revd Canon Walter Asbil	2	ACC-8
	*Mrs Patricia Bays	3C	ACC-7
Central Africa	The Very Revd Robert A B Ewbank (replaced at 1987 meeting by The Revd Bernard Malango)	3	ACC-9
	Mr Gervaise Chidawanyika	1	ACC-7
Ceylon	The Rt Revd Andrew Kumarage Bishop of Kurunagala	2	ACC-9
East Asia	The Rt Revd Luke Chhoa Bishop of Sabah	2	ACC-8
	* # The Ven Yong Ping Chung		ACC-8
	Mrs Alice Chong Yuk Tan-Fun (replaced at 1987 meeting by Mr Louis Tsui)	4	ACC-9
England	The Rt Revd Colin W James Bishop of Winchester	2	ACC-9
	# *The Revd Canon Colin Craston	1C	ACC-9
	Dr Margaret Hewitt (replaced at 1987 meeting by Mr John Smallwood)	1	ACC-9
Indian Ocean	The Most Revd French K Chang-Him Bishop of the Seychelles and Archbishop of the Indian Ocean	2	ACC-7

Ireland	* # The Most Revd Robert H A Eames Archbishop of Armagh and Primate of All Ireland	3	ACC-8
	Mr J L Barry Deane	4	ACC-7
Japan	* # The Rt Revd Joseph J Iida	3	ACC-8
Jerusalem and the Middle East	Mr Ibrahim Wakid	3	ACC-7
Kenya	The Rt Revd David Gitari Bishop of Mount Kenya East	4	ACC-9
	Mrs Rhoda Lusaka	2	ACC-8
Melanesia	The Most Revd Norman Palmer Bishop of Central Melanesia and Archbishop of Melanesia (replaced at 1987 meeting by Mr John Tealiklava)	4	ACC-7
New Zealand	The Most Revd Brian Davis Bishop of Wellington and Archbishop of New Zealand	2	ACC-7
	# Mr Edgar Bradley	3	ACC-9
Nigeria	The Rt Rev Samuel Ebo Bishop of Okigwe/Orlu	4	ACC-8
	The Very Revd Samuel Johnson	1	ACC-7
	Mr Justice Christian Abimbola	2	ACC-9
North India	The Most Revd Din Dayal Bishop of Lucknow and Moderator of the Church of North India	4	ACC-8
Pakistan	The Rt Revd Arne Rudvin Bishop of Karachi	3	ACC-7
Papua New Guinea	Mr Gideon Waida	2	ACC-7
Scotland	The Revd Canon Ian Watt	1	ACC-9
Southern Africa	The Rt Revd Lawrence Zulu Bishop of Zululand	2	ACC-7
	* # The Revd Canon Winston Ndungane	1	ACC-8
	Mrs Betty Govinden	4	ACC-9
South America	# Dr Julio Lozano	4	ACC-9

South India	The Most Revd I Jesudasan Bishop of South Kerala and Moderator of the Church of South India	3	ACC-7
Sudan	The Rt Revd Daniel Zindo Bishop of Yambio	4	ACC-9
	The Revd John Kanyikwa	1	ACC-8
Tanzania	The Most Revd John Ramadhani Bishop of Zanzibar and Tanga and Archbishop of Tanzania	3	ACC-7
	The Revd Canon Simon Chiwanga	4C	ACC-8
Uganda	The Rt Revd Benoni Ogwal-Abwang Bishop of Northern Uganda (replaced at 1987 meeting by The Rt Revd Cyprian Bamwoze Bishop of Busoga)	1	ACC-9
	*The Revd Canon Benezeri Kisembo	4	ACC-7
	Professor Enoka Rukare	3	ACC-7
USA	The Most Revd Edmond L Browning Presiding Bishop of ECUSA	1	ACC-8
	The Very Revd Frederick Borsch	2	ACC-7
	# Mrs Pamela Chinnis	3	ACC-10
Wales	The Most Revd George Noakes Bishop of St David's and Archbishop of Wales	3	ACC-9
	Mr J W David McIntyre	1	ACC-8
West Africa	*# The Most Revd George D Browne Bishop of Liberia and Archbishop of West Africa	2C	ACC-8
West Indies	The Rt Revd Drexel W Gomez Bishop of Barbados	4	ACC-8
	The Revd David Benjamin	3	ACC-7
Co-opted	The Most Revd Richard A Abellon Bishop of the Northern Philippines and Prime Bishop of the Philippine Episcopal Church	3	ACC-8
	Mrs Ruth Yangsoon-Choi Korea	1	ACC-9
	Mrs Faga Matalavea Western Samoa	4	ACC-9

Miss Lorna Helen Ireland	2	ACC-9
The Rt Revd James H Ottley Bishop of Panama	4	ACC-9

PARTICIPANTS FROM CHURCHES IN FULL COMMUNION

Mar Thoma Syrian Church of Malabar	The Rt Revd Philipose Mar Chrysostom Suffragan Metropolitan of the Mar Thoma Church
Old Catholic Church	The Rt Revd Gerhard A Van Kleef Bishop of Haarlem

PARTICIPANTS FROM OTHER CHURCHES

Lutheran Church	The Revd Dr Jonas Jonson
Orthodox Church	The Revd Dr John Chryssavgis Archdiocese of Australia
Roman Catholic Church	The Revd Kevin McDonald Vatican Secretariat for Promoting Christian Unity
World Alliance of Reformed Churches	The Revd Dr Stephen C Tan Singapore
World Council of Churches	Mr William P Thompson USA

CONSULTANTS

Section I	The Revd Pritam B Santram, India
Section II	Professor Nicholas Lash, England
Section III	The Revd Dr Harding Meyer, France Dr George Ninan, Christian Conference of Asia
Section IV	The Revd Dr Allan Boesak, South Africa The Revd Charles Cesaretti, USA

ACC-7 SECTION SECRETARIES

Section I	The Rt Revd Kenneth Mason, Australia
Section II	The Revd Richard Harries, England (since consecrated Bishop of Oxford)

Section III   The Revd Canon Christopher Hill, England
Section IV   The Ven. Alan Nichols, Australia

ACC-7 STAFF

The Revd George Braund
Mr Robert Byers
Mrs Christine Codner
The Revd Stephen Commins
Miss Flavia Gonsalves
Miss Deirdre Hoban
Mr David Long
The Revd Canon Martin Mbwana
Miss Emma Morgan
The Rt Revd Michael Nazir-Ali
The Revd Canon Howard Root
The Revd Michael Sams
The Revd Canon Roger Symon
Ms Vanessa Wilde

ACC-7 COMMUNICATION TEAM

The Revd John Barton, England
The Revd Peter Davis, New Zealand
The Revd Charles Long, USA
Mrs Ruth Nicastro, USA
Miss Susan Young, England
Mr Stephen Webb, Australia

PREVIOUS MEETINGS OF THE COUNCIL

ACC-1   Limuru, Kenya, 23 February-5March 1971
Report *The Time is Now* (out of print)

ACC-2   Dublin, Ireland, 17-27 July, 1973
Report *Partners in Mission*

ACC-3   Trinidad, 23 March-2 April, 1976
Report *ACC-3 Trinidad*

ACC-4   London, Ontario, Canada, 8-18 May 1979
Report of the Fourth Meeting 1979

ACC-5   Newcastle, England, 8-18 September 1981
Report of Fifth Meeting

ACC-6   Badagry, Nigeria, 17-27 July 1984
Report *Bonds of Affection*

(Available from Anglican Consultative Council, 14 Great Peter Street, London SW1P 3NQ, England.

ABBREVIATIONS USED IN THIS REPORT

ACC	Anglican Consultative Council
AIDS	Acquired Immune Deficiency Syndrome
ARCIC I	Anglican Roman Catholic International Commission
ARCIC II	Anglican Roman Catholic International Commission II
BBC	British Broadcasting Corporation
BEM	Baptism, Eucharist and Ministry, published by the World Council of Churches
CESA	Church of England in South Africa
CPSA	Church of the Province of Southern Africa
IAIN	Inter-Anglican Information Network
MISAG	Mission Issues and Strategy Advisory Group
MISAG 2	Mission Issues and Strategy Advisory Group 2
NGO	Non Governmental Organisation (a United Nations designation)
OPEC	Organisation of Petroleum Exporting Countries
PLO	Palestinian Liberation Organisation
PIM	Partners in Mission
SPCK	Society for the Promotion of Christian Knowledge
USPG	United Society for the Propagation of the Gospel
WCC	World Council of Churches

PUBLICATIONS AND REPORTS ASSOCIATED WITH THIS REPORT

The following publications are available through the Inter-Anglican Publishing Network:

For the Sake of the Kingdom The Report of the Inter-Anglican Theological and Doctrinal Commission

Towards a Theology for Inter-Faith Dialogue

Salvation and the Church (ARCIC II)

Open to the Spirit

Authority in the Anglican Communion

Peace and Justice – A Working Paper

Transforming Families and Communities

The Emmaus Report

Other documents referred to:

Giving Mission Its Proper Place (ACC)

Progress in Partnership (ACC)

Equal Partners (AIO Sydney)

Light from the East (ABC Toronto)

ARCIC The Final Report (SPCK)

Anglican-Orthodox Dialogue The Dublin Agreed Statement 1984 (SPCK)

God's Reign and Our Unity (SPCK)

Index

Australia
Anglican Information Office
St Andrew's House
Sydney Square
Sydney 2000

Canada
Anglican Book Centre
600 Jarvis Street
Toronto, Ontario M4Y 2J6

Ghana
Anglican Press Ltd
PO Box 8
Accra

India
ISPCK
PO BOX 1585
Kashmere Gate, Delhi 11006

Kenya
Uzima Press Ltd
PO Box 48127
Nairobi

New Zealand
Collins Liturgical Publications
PO Box 1
31 Viewfield Road
Auckland

Nigeria
CSS Press
50 Broad Street
PO Box 174
Lagos

Southern and Central Africa
Collins Liturgical Publications
Distributed in
Southern Africa by
Lux Verbi, PO Box 1822
Cape Town 80000

Tanzania
Central Tanganyika Press
PO Box 15
Dodoma

Uganda
Centenary Publishing House
PO Box 2776
Kampala

United Kingdom
Church House Publishing
Church House
Great Smith Street
London SW1P 3NZ

United States of America
Forward Movement Publications
412 Sycamore Street
Cincinnati, Ohio 45202

Member Churches of the ACC

The Anglican Church of Australia
The Episcopal Church of Brazil
The Church of the Province of Burma
The Church of the Province of Burundi, Rwanda and Zaire
The Anglican Church of Canada
The Church of the Province of Central Africa
The Church of Ceylon
The Council of the Churches of East Asia
The Church of England
The Church of the Province of the Indian Ocean
The Church of Ireland
The Holy Catholic Church in Japan
The Episcopal Church in Jerusalem and the Middle East
The Church of the Province of Kenya
The Church of the Province of Melanesia
The Church of the Province of New Zealand
The Church of the Province of Nigeria
The Anglican Church of Papua New Guinea
The Scottish Episcopal Church
The Church of the Province of Southern Africa
The Anglican Church of the Southern Cone of America
The Episcopal Church of the Sudan
The Church of the Province of Tanzania
The Church of the Province of Uganda
The Episcopal Church in the United States of America
The Church in Wales
The Church of the Province of West Africa
The Church in the Province of the West Indies
The Church of North India
The Church of South India
The Church of Pakistan

Member Churches of the ACC